BRITAIN IN THE
EUROPEAN COMMUNITY

ANDREW GEDDES

baseline
BOOKS

First published 1993 by
Baseline Book Company
PO Box 34
Chorlton
Manchester M21 1LL

British Library Cataloguing in Publication Data

ISBN 1 897626 02 9

Cover design   Ian Price
Cover illustration   Min Cooper
Typesetting   Kathryn Holliday
Printed and bound by Nuffield Press, Oxford

ACKNOWLEDGEMENTS

I am grateful to Ian Holliday and Mike Goldsmith for helpful comments. Any errors of fact or interpretation that remain are of course my responsibility. **AG**

CONTENTS

TABLES

ABBREVIATIONS

ASEAN	Association of South East Asian Nations
AUEW	Amalgamated Union of Engineering Workers
CAP	Common Agricultural Policy
CBI	Confederation of British Industry
CFSP	Common Foreign and Security Policy
COPA	Committee of Professional Agricultural Associations
COREPER	Committee of Permanent Representatives
DM	Deutschmark
DUP	Democratic Unionist Party (Northern Ireland)
EAGGF	European Agricultural Guidance and Guarantee Fund
EC	European Community
ECHR	European Convention on Human Rights
ECJ	European Court of Justice
ECOFIN	Economics and Finance Ministers' Council
ECSC	European Coal and Steel Community
Ecu	European Currency Unit
EDC	European Defence Community
EEA	European Economic Area
EEC	European Economic Community
EFTA	European Free Trade Association
EMS	European Monetary System
EMU	Economic and Monetary Union
EPC	European Political Cooperation
EPP	European People's Party
ERDF	European Regional Development Fund
ERM	Exchange Rate Mechanism
ESF	European Social Fund
ETUC	European Trades Union Congress
EUF	European Union of Federalists
Euratom	European Atomic Energy Community
FRG	Federal Republic of Germany
GATT	General Agreement on Tariffs and Trade
GDP	Gross Domestic Product
GDR	German Democratic Republic
GNP	Gross National Product
IGC	Intergovernmental Conference
JHA	Justice and Home Affairs Policy

MAFF	Ministry of Agriculture, Fisheries and Food
NAFTA	North American Free-Trade Agreement
NATO	North Atlantic Treaty Organisation
NFU	National Farmers' Union
NWRA	North West Regional Association
OEEC	Organisation for European Economic Cooperation
OUP	Ulster ('Official') Unionist Party (Northern Ireland)
PR	Proportional Representation
QMV	Qualified Majority Voting
SDLP	Social Democratic and Labour Party (Northern Ireland)
SDP	Social Democratic Party
SEA	Single European Act
SNP	Scottish National Party
TUC	Trades Union Congress
TUPE	Transfer of Undertakings (Protection of Employment)
UKREP	UK Permanent Representation to the EC
UNICE	Union of Industries of the EC
VAT	Value Added Tax
WEU	West European Union

INTRODUCTION

Love it, loathe it or feel totally indifferent about it, one cannot deny the central role that the European Community (EC) plays in the modern world. Established in a continent divided by ideology into two hostile camps, the EC has recently witnessed the collapse of its Communist competitor to the east. Since 1989 it has faced problems generated not by ideology but by the rivalries of distinct trading blocs in a new world order. In future years its strongest challenges are likely to come from powerful Pacific Rim economies, such as Japan and South Korea, which form the Association of South East Asian Nations (ASEAN), and from the North American Free-Trade Agreement (NAFTA), comprising the USA, Canada and Mexico. However, unlike regional organisations in South East Asia and North America, the EC is supranational. In certain areas, such as trade and agriculture, its member states have ceded power – or 'sovereignty' – to Community-level institutions to make decisions which are binding on them. This supranationalism is both a central and a controversial aspect of the EC. Its implications for Britain are the focus of this book.

BRITAIN IN THE EUROPEAN COMMUNITY

Britain distrusted the supranational aspirations of the nascent Community in the 1950s and since it joined the EC in 1973 has acquired the reputation of being a reluctant European. Whether this is justified can only be determined by looking both at British policy towards the Community and at how Community membership has affected Britain.

Membership of the European Community has had an extensive impact on British politics, economy and society. Responsibility for important policy sectors has been transferred to EC institutions. As power has been ceded to the Community so political activity has been refocused. Government ministers frequently meet with colleagues from other member states in EC decision-making forums. Some pressure groups now look to Brussels as much as to Whitehall. Consequently, it is important to understand the workings of EC institutions and not to regard the Community simply as a 'foreign policy' issue. Its remit stretches to a wide range of domestic activities.

However, although Britain is now deeply involved in the EC, it is important not to exaggerate its centrality to the Community. Britain, for a variety of reasons, has always been peripheral to the integrative process which has characterised EC history. Having been the leading European nation at the end of World War Two, Britain has become increasingly marginalised in subsequent years. When John Major became prime minister in November 1990, he expressed the intention of reversing this state of affairs by once again placing Britain 'at the heart of Europe'. Yet whether Britain can move towards a central position in the Community in the 1990s remains an open question.

EC FACTS AND FIGURES

The EC is both an economic and a political entity, and seeks integration at both levels. The precise link between these two processes is, however, a matter of great contention. Some argue that economic integration should be separated from political. Others maintain that no such separation is possible. Underlying this debate is an undeniable drive towards economic integration in Europe. All statistics show that the EC is increasingly becoming a single economic area.

There are currently 12 members of the EC. Its founders were France, West Germany, Italy, Belgium, the Netherlands and Luxembourg. In 1951 these six countries signed the Treaty of Paris which established the European Coal and Steel Community (ECSC). In 1957 they signed the Treaties of Rome which created the European Economic Community (EEC) – or Common Market – and the European Atomic Energy Community (Euratom).

These three Communities are now usually referred to in the singular as the European Community. In 1973 Britain, Ireland and Denmark joined, to be followed in 1981 by Greece and in 1986 by Portugal and Spain. The Maastricht Treaty, signed in February 1992 and due for ratification by the end of 1993, creates a European Union. Citizens of all 12 member states are also citizens of the new Union.

Total EC population in 1993 is just over 350 million (Table 0.1, opposite), the largest member country being the reunified Germany created in 1991 following collapse of the German Democratic Republic (GDR). For comparison, the USA has a population of 260 million, and Japan a population of 125 million.

Table 0.1 Population of the European Community, 1993

	Millions
Belgium	10.0
Denmark	5.2
France	57.9
Germany	81.6
Greece	10.4
Ireland	3.6
Italy	58.0
Luxembourg	0.4
Netherlands	15.3
Portugal	9.4
Spain	39.1
UK	59.9
EC12	**350.8**

Source *European Economy* (OOP, Luxembourg, 1993)

A salient characteristic of the EC is intensification throughout its history of trading links between member states (Table 0.2). In 1958 Britain exported just over one-fifth of its products to the countries which were later to be its EC partners. A little more than 30 years later, in 1991, this proportion had increased to well over half. The pattern of imports from EC countries developed almost as much over the same period.

Table 0.2 Trading links within the EC, 1958-91

	Exports from other EC members		Imports from other EC members	
	1958	1991	1958	1991
Belgium/Lux	55.4	75.2	55.5	70.5
Denmark	59.3	54.1	60.0	54.2
Germany	37.9	53.8	36.3	54.5
Greece	50.9	63.5	53.7	60.3
Spain	46.8	66.4	31.8	59.8
France	30.9	63.6	28.3	64.2
Ireland	82.4	74.4	68.9	69.1
Italy	34.5	59.0	30.2	57.7
Netherlands	58.3	76.2	50.7	59.0
Portugal	38.9	75.1	53.4	71.9
UK	21.7	56.3	21.8	50.1
EC12	**37.2**	**61.6**	**35.2**	**58.6**

Source Ibid

The web of interdependence created by ever stronger trading links means that the economic health of individual member states depends increasingly on the prosperity of their Community partners. Consequently prosperity becomes a collective endeavour. However, the strengthening of trading links within the EC has not helped overcome the cyclical nature of capitalist economic development. The founder members of the Community enjoyed high levels of economic growth. Indeed, Dutch Nobel prize-winning economist Jan Tinbergen was moved to observe in the early 1960s that Western economies would henceforth enjoy 'festoons' of economic growth. Many linked this prosperity to integration within the European Community. However, the oil price increases in the 1970s showed this optimism to be misplaced. Between 1974 and 1984 annual economic growth in the Community averaged only 1.9 per cent.

Unfortunately for the British they joined the EC in 1973 at the very moment when the economies of the Community entered recession and the integrative process moved into a period of stagnation. This raised doubts, not least in Britain, about the effectiveness of the Community. A further major recession in the early 1990s, during which unemployment has risen to very high levels (Table 0.3), has prompted similar doubts. As the Community becomes central to member state economies so economic problems tend to be laid at the door of the Community. Support for integration dwindles during hard times.

Table 0.3 EC Unemployment, 1993[1]

	Total in millions	Percentage of workforce
Belgium	0.520	9.3
Denmark	0.363	9.5
Germany	2.288	6.0
Greece	0.213	8.5
Spain	2.471	19.5
France	3.098	10.8
Ireland	2.996	19.2
Italy	4.450	10.6
Luxembourg	0.003	2.0
Netherlands	0.368	7.6
Portugal	0.359	5.4
UK	3.043	12.3
EC12	**17.475**	**10.6**

1 February
Source Ibid

Yet there is no doubt that membership of the EC has been linked in the past with high growth rates. Whether there is a relationship of cause and effect here is of course disputable. Table 0.4 shows GDP per capita 1958-92 for Community members. The relative economic decline of Britain is striking. From being the second richest state in 1960, Britain had slipped to eighth richest by 1990. This relative decline began before Britain gained membership of the Community, and has not been arrested since.

Table 0.4 GDP per capita in EC member states, 1960-90[1]

	1960	1970	1980	1990
Belgium	115.4	115.0	121.7	104.9
Denmark	123.2	140.1	131.4	137.9
Germany	123.8	133.3	134.2	129.2
Greece	39.8	49.5	42.3	35.3
Spain	36.3	49.1	58.3	68.4
France	126.9	123.4	125.2	113.9
Ireland	59.1	57.4	57.4	65.3
Italy	75.2	87.1	81.5	102.1
Luxembourg	158.0	142.7	126.7	124.5
Netherlands	97.0	112.2	121.6	100.9
Portugal	28.0	32.2	27.4	33.1
UK	**131.1**	**97.0**	**96.9**	**94.0**

1 Calculated at current market prices; EC=100
Source Ibid

Relatively high economic growth has made the EC one of the most powerful economic blocs in the world, and one of the most important markets. They are a major reason for expansion of the Community in the 1970s and 1980s, and for the current queue of applicants. Yet the gains of membership secured by Britain remain unclear.

BRITISH MEMBERSHIP ASSESSED

The central aim of this book is to assess British membership of the EC, which has now lasted for more than 20 years. It begins by introducing the terminology of European integration. Chapter 1 explains many of the terms used by analysts of European integration – including supra-nationalism, intergovernmentalism, sovereignty and federalism – and looks at ways in which the use of such terminology can inform an assessment of Britain's EC membership.

Chapter 2 focuses on the historical origins of the Community and the emergence of the ECSC, Euratom and the EEC in the 1950s. It also examines the failure to create a European Defence Community in 1954. Chapter 3 appraises the policy of successive British governments towards the Community. It asks why Britain did not join the Community in the 1950s and why Britain then decided to seek entry in the 1960s. The policies of successive British governments since 1973 – from Edward Heath's to John Major's – are then appraised.

Chapter 4 analyses the institutional structure of the European Community. It looks at the power and responsibilities of the Commission, the Council of Ministers, the European Parliament, the Court of Justice and the European Council. It also asks whether there is a 'democratic deficit' in the EC. The Maastricht Treaty is the focus of Chapter 5. Its implications for European integration are assessed through analysis of prospects for economic and monetary union, for Community social policy and for cooperation in defence, security and home affairs amongst EC member states.

Chapter 6 examines the policy responsibilities of the Community. It looks at principal areas of activity such as agriculture and regional aid, and also assesses some of the more day-to-day implications of Community membership for people in Britain. Chapter 7 surveys the likelihood of new members entering the Community in the 1990s, and also considers prospects for further integration. Chapter 8 looks at the myriad influences on British political and economic life of Community membership and asks how well integrated into the EC Britain has become. The Conclusion speculates on future development of the Community and Britain's role in it.

Debates about the EC and its integrative potential have a habit of generating more heat than light. The chapters that follow seek to illuminate some of the more salient features of an organisation that has become central to political and economic life in Britain.

1 EUROSPEAK

European integration provokes both fervent support and deep mistrust. Yet key terms used in debates about integration are often obscure or misunderstood. The first task in any discussion of Britain and the EC is therefore to acquire a basic understanding of the meaning of terms such as integration, supranationalism, sovereignty and federalism. Later chapters will show that Britain's preference has always been for intergovernmentalism. Consequently, supranationalism has always been viewed with great wariness.

INTEGRATION

A conceptual framework – a way of thinking – about European integration is needed. Otherwise any analysis is no more than a collection of dates and facts within which assumptions about the nature of the integrative process remain implicit and obscured rather than explicit and explained.

Indeed, the very meaning of Europe also needs to be made clear: 'there is no single or agreed Europe'.[1] This book analyses the 12 EC member states. The EC emerged during the Cold War and is composed of capitalist economies in western Europe. In the 1990s, following the collapse of the Soviet bloc, it faces the challenge of responding to the 'new Europe'. This immediately makes the point that the EC and Europe are not one and the same thing. The two terms cannot be transposed. Within the wider Europe a complex web of interdependent states and markets cooperate in an array of organisations. What is significant about the EC, and distinguishes it from other organisations, is that it is supranational. This term will itself be analysed later in this chapter.

Integration, according to the American analyst Ernst Haas, is 'a process for the creation of political communities' within which 'states cease to be wholly sovereign'.[2] In post-war Europe the main drive has been towards creation of structures to promote *economic integration*. Such integration can be divided into five main types:[3]

- A **free trade area** within which tariffs and quotas are eliminated between member countries
- A **customs union** within which tariffs and quotas are removed and an external tariff is imposed on goods and services entering the union
- A **common market** within which people, goods, services, and capital can move freely
- An **economic and monetary union** involving a single currency and harmonisation of some national economic policies
- **Total economic integration** whereby the same economic policies are pursued in all the member states.

In the 1950s Britain preferred to limit itself to the first of these five levels of integration. In July 1959 it established the European Free Trade Area (EFTA) with six other countries (Austria, Denmark, Norway, Portugal, Sweden and Switzerland). Britain, like many of its EFTA partners, was fearful of the implications for national sovereignty of the EC, which was a customs union and had a series of supranational structures. In subsequent years, many of the EFTA countries nevertheless lodged applications to join. In 1986 the Single European Act set the EC on course for the third level of economic integration – a common, or single, market – within which people, goods, services, and capital should be able to move freely. The single European market officially came into being on 1 January 1993, though it has not yet been perfected. In 1991 the Maastricht Treaty embodied plans for progress towards the fourth level – economic and monetary union – which is supposedly to be attained by the end of this century.

Economic integration and the interdependence it generates may create pressure for political integration. There are four aspects to this:[4]
- **Institutional integration**, comprising the growth of collective decision-making structures with common institutions and formal rules
- **Policy integration** whereby responsibility for particular policies is transferred to the supranational level
- **Attitudinal integration** which involves growth of support amongst the peoples of the participating countries
- **Security integration**, whereby states come to expect non-violent relations.

There is clear evidence of institutional and policy integration in the EC with the development of common institutions such as the European Commission and the European Parliament and common policies such as the Common Agricultural Policy (CAP). There has also been steady growth in support for the EC amongst the people of the Community (see Chapter 8). However, few will be unfamiliar with the events of 1992 when the people of Denmark rejected the Maastricht Treaty in a referendum: in June 1992 51 per cent voted 'No', 49 per cent voted 'Yes'. The people of France almost voted similarly, delivering no more than a *petit oui* to Maastricht: here in September 1992 51 per cent voted 'Yes', 49 per cent voted 'No'.

Part of the problem is that the process of European integration tends to be driven by political and economic élites. Despite the founding Treaties' aspiration to create 'a closer union of the peoples of Europe', many EC institutions can seem distant from the people whose interests they are supposed to serve. There is talk of a 'democratic deficit' in the European Community, an absence of democracy and accountability which prevents it from acquiring the political legitimacy necessary to attitudinal integration.

When it comes to security integration it is important to note the strong Atlanticist tinge given to the defence of western Europe by the North Atlantic Treaty Organisation (NATO). It was America that, by and large, provided the security umbrella for the liberal democracies of western Europe during the Cold War. In these years Atlanticism, not Europeanism, shaped the collective defence structures of western Europe. Even now it remains an important aspect of EC thinking.

SUPRANATIONALISM

Britain chose not to participate in creation of the EC in the 1950s. One of the reasons for this was a deep distrust of the aspirations of the EC. Britain did not favour supranationalism because it feared the implications for national sovereignty. The EC is a good example of supranationalism, whereby formal structures of government are established above the nation state. There are three key features of supranational government:[5]
● The institutions of the supranational government are independent from those of member states
● The organisation can make rules that bind members and has the power to enforce those rules
● The institutions of the supranational government are part of a new legal system to which member states and individuals are subject.

EC law over-rides national law, and institutions exist at the supranational (EC) level that are independent of member states. Supranational government has clear implications for traditional notions of national sovereignty. National sovereignty means that a country has supreme authority within its territory. Any country that is bound by the rules of a supranational organisation no longer has supreme authority, and is therefore no longer fully sovereign.

Britain has always preferred *intergovernmental cooperation* to supranational government. Intergovernmentalism implies unanimity as the basis of decision-making, and allows a veto to be exercised to protect national interests. However, the founders of the EC – France, Germany, Italy and the Benelux countries – were suspicious of political systems based on the notion of a national veto, and sought to move away from intergovernmentalism. They pointed to the intergovernmental League of Nations which, in the inter-war period, was for a number of reasons unable to exert the authority necessary to prevent drift towards World War Two.

SOVEREIGNTY

A sovereign state holds and exercises supreme authority within its territorial jurisdiction. For many years, the United Kingdom of Great Britain and Northern Ireland was a sovereign state. However, any country which signs up to a supranational body of law, such as that which established the EC, is compromising its national sovereignty because law which is determined collectively over-rides that which it creates itself. EC law is binding on its member states.

In Britain sovereign authority is vested in Parliament. The British constitution can be summed up in six words: what the monarch in Parliament decides. By joining the EC the British Parliament reduced its own sovereignty because in some areas it is supranational institutions of the EC that make laws.

Opponents of the EC argue that loss of sovereignty in a democratic political system reduces the rights of citizens to exercise control over decision-making authority. The ultimate recourse of the British electorate is to 'kick the rascals out' by voting for a change of government at a general election. However, if the national government is no longer the sovereign authority then national elections and policy preferences expressed in them may make little difference if they run counter to preferences agreed at Community level.

Advocates of European integration argue that sovereignty is not a static concept to be jealously guarded. Rather, it is to be utilised to the greatest benefits of the citizens of a particular state. Membership of the EC means that sovereignty is 'pooled' at supranational level in some policy areas, such as trade, where it can be utilised more effectively. To put it simply, 12 are stronger than one, and are far more likely to secure beneficial results for Community citizens than are the unilateral actions of one country.

The issue of sovereignty – or as Margaret Thatcher prefers to put it 'who decides' – has been central to Britain's relationship with the Community. There is, however, an important distinction to be made between *formal* and *informal* aspects of sovereignty:

> ... it has been the formal and visible transfer of sovereignty embodied in the issue of UK membership of the EC which has provided the main focus for public concern ... Successive British governments have taken a pragmatic, even a relaxed attitude to the informal processes of international interdependence, and the consequent erosion of national sovereignty.[6]

The point is that to focus on formal aspects of sovereignty, such as supposed Parliamentary supremacy, may be to neglect disguised informal transfers of sovereignty that heighten Britain's interdependence within the international economic and political order. Formally, Britain was still a sovereign nation before it joined the EC in 1973. Yet informally it was losing sovereignty on an annual basis as processes of economic integration in an increasingly interdependent world reduced its real control over its own affairs.

Indeed, the MacDonald government had found itself largely at the mercy of international financiers in 1931, and the Wilson government had been similarly embarrassed in 1967 when devaluation of the pound was forced. Even in 1973, then, it could hardly be argued that Britain was in all senses a 'sovereign' nation. In years since then the point has been made ever more clearly. Ironically, Thatcher may have hastened processes of informal integration by relaxing exchange controls in 1979, thereby removing a potential power from the armoury of British government. Even when sterling 'floated' out of the EC's

Exchange Rate Mechanism (ERM) in September 1992 Britain found that its economic policy continued to be greatly influenced by decisions taken by the German Bundesbank.

The issues of supranationalism and sovereignty lead directly to consideration of the dreaded 'F-word': federalism.

FEDERALISM

In earlier ages Britain, through plans drawn up for former colonies, was one of the world's great federalisers.[7] However, British governments have consistently seen federation as appropriate for others, not for the British. The British system of government is *unitary*: local government is subordinate to central. In Britain local government only exists because central government gives it tasks and responsibilities, and as it gives those tasks so it can take them away.

In federal systems, such as the United States and Germany, neither the central nor the regional level of government is supposed to be subordinate to the other. Federalism is seen as generating effective central power for handling common problems whilst preserving regional autonomy. Five main features of a federal system of government can be highlighted:[8]

● Two levels of government, a general and a regional
● Formal distribution of legislative and executive authority and sources of revenue between the two levels
● A written constitution
● An umpire – a supreme or constitutional court – to adjudicate in disputes between the two levels
● Central institutions, including a bicameral legislature within which the upper chamber will usually embody territorial representation, as in the case with the US Senate and the German Bundesrat.

In the EC there are some signs of federation. Clearly there are two levels of government (in fact more), each of which has its own budgetary resources. In addition, an established body of European law over-rides national law. The European Court of Justice (ECJ) acts as umpire in disputes between supranational and national levels of government. Bulmer and Wessels argue that what is emerging is a system of 'cooperative federalism': Community and national governments share responsibility for problem-solving because neither of them has the legal authority or policy competence to tackle the challenges that they face on their own.[9]

In Britain opponents of a 'federal Europe' use the term in a way markedly different to the meaning given to it by most federalists. For its opponents a 'federal Europe' means a European superstate with a huge centralised Brussels bureaucracy limiting the sovereign authority of member states. Advocates, on the other hand, see federation as a way of combining the political virtues of unity and diversity. For them, federalism is a means of decentralising power, not centralising it.

SUBSIDIARITY

Resolution of the dispute between federalists and anti-federalists depends in large measure on questions of detail. The key is to decide which powers are to go to which level, supranational, national or regional. In the late 1980s and the early 1990s the EC has been keen to proceed on the basis of *subsidiarity*, maintaining that power should be exercised at the lowest appropriate level. Subsidiarity is a rather amorphous notion and is one of the words used in debates on the European Community that baffles people as much as it informs them. In 1992 Commission President Jacques Delors offered a job and Ecu 200 000 to anyone who could define subsidiarity in one page.

The word originates from the Latin *subsidium*, meaning reserve troops. It first appeared in Pope Leo XIII's 1891 encyclical. In 1931 Pope Pius XI used it to denote that political and social decisions should not be taken at a higher level than necessary. The EC's leaders seized on the principle in the late 1980s, seeing it as a way of bridging the gap between the people and the Community. Lawyers, though, warned of the dangers of taking a religious principle and converting it into a legal text.

British Prime Minister, John Major, portrays subsidiarity as implying a division of responsibility between the EC and member states, with member states holding the upper hand. The problem for the British government may be that subsidiarity can also mean powers going to lower levels of government than the national state. This could necessitate a transfer of power to regions or, in Britain, the sub-state nations of Scotland and Wales. Germans tend to see subsidiarity as meaning a distribution of power between regions (*Länder*), Bonn and

Brussels. French President Mitterrand insists that subsidiarity should not weaken the Community or involve a repatriation of powers. Smaller countries, such as the Netherlands, Belgium and Luxembourg have been determined to block any reduction in the powers of the Commission which they believe gives a voice to smaller member states. The Birmingham Summit meeting of EC heads' of government in October 1992 agreed that the Community would only act where it was 'proper and necessary' and obliged the Commission to incorporate a subsidiarity justification in future legislative proposals.

Regionalists seek a 'Europe of the regions' with nation states by-passed as powers move down to the local level and up to the EC.[10] The Commission has been active in encouraging links between regions and the EC and between regions themselves, especially those that straddle borders. The European Parliament's 1988 Charter of the Regions is a further indication of the importance supranational institutions give to the fostering of regional identities within the Community. The Maastricht Treaty establishes an advisory Committee of the Regions with 189 members.

NEO-FUNCTIONALISM

If there are signs of federation in the EC, then what forces are driving this process? Why has integration occurred? In the wake of the devastation wrought by World War Two the European Union of Federalists (EUF) was established. Many of its members had fought in the resistance against the Nazis. The EUF did not think it too far-fetched to hope that a United States of Europe could emerge to shape post-war Europe. For them maintenance of a system of nation states would very probably continue to breed the nationalist politics that had been responsible for two world wars in the first half of the twentieth century. However, advocates of constitutional federalism were to see their dreams overtaken by events. Nation states were soon restored to Europe, and advocates of closer integration sought an alternative approach.

This alternative approach was exemplified by the Schuman Plan of 1950 – Robert Schuman was French foreign minister – which led to creation of the ECSC in 1951. This was the forerunner of the EC. The ECSC established a common market in coal and steel, both key areas for industrial economies. However, Schuman planned far more than a mere coal and steel community. He saw the ECSC as a first step on the road to economic and political integration in Europe. Schuman hoped that successful integration in one area would create pressure for integration in other areas. For example, a common market for coal and steel would create pressure for broader cooperation in energy policies. This, in turn, would create pressure for cooperation in industrial policies. In this way an initially small step would snowball.

Students of integration describe this snowballing as a 'spillover effect', with cooperation in one area creating pressure for integration in others. This inexorable logic is known as *neo-functionalist spillover*.[11] It was expected that this spillover effect would be generated at the supranational level with the Commission, much to the delight of new Eurocrats, in the lead. As integration continued apace then functions that had previously been performed by member states would pass to the supranational level where they could be more effectively performed. This functional spillover would also generate a political spillover as there would be a re-focusing of activity, for example by pressure groups, on newly-important supranational institutions.

This sounded plausible and appeared to fit EC development in the 1950s and early 1960s. However, the theory no longer seemed applicable in the period from the mid 1960s to the mid 1980s. In 1965 French President de Gaulle enforced national rights of veto in EC decision-making, thereby reducing the scope of supranational authority. During the 1970s the EC seemed incapable of acting during severe economic recession. On 20 March 1982 the *Economist*'s front cover showed a tombstone bearing an inscription for the EC. It read:

EEC
Born March 25, 1957
Moribund March 25, 1982
Capax imperii nisi imperasset [it seemed capable of power until it tried to wield it].

At this time the momentum of the integrative process appeared to have dissipated. 'Eurosclerosis' was widely held to have set in. Not surprisingly, neo-functionalist theories fell into obsolescence.

THE OBSOLESCENCE OF INTEGRATION THEORY?

George claims that an erroneous 'end of ideology' assumption under-pinned neo-functionalist theory. It implied that economic growth would continue unabated, and that the main question facing western societies was how to distribute the fruits of this wealth.[12] Neo-functionalists thought that the best way to do it was by appointing experts – technocrats – at the supranational level who, because of their expertise, would arrive at decisions that were best for everybody. It did not quite work out like that. In the 1970s governments were faced with the problem of coping with both rising unemployment and increasing inflation. Supranational integration was not an option many appeared to consider.

George also argues that neo-functionalists tried to write nationalism out of the political equation. They thought that nationalist views would be consigned to history, overwhelmed by the logic of integra-tion. Again this was not to be the case. In the 1960s the EC came into conflict with strongly nationalistic Gaullists in France, in the 1980s with Thatcherites in Britain. As Wallace writes, 'Politics follows its own logic, not simply those of economics and technology'.[13] Nationalists like Charles de Gaulle and Margaret Thatcher would not be swept along by the 'inexorable logic' of integration.

How then do we explain the resurgence of integration that occurred in the mid 1980s? It would seem strange to try to breathe new life into neo-functionalist theory when it appears to have failed to explain events from 1965 until 1984. Analysts have instead pointed to the importance of member states in the process of integration.

'REALIST' VIEWS

In creating a spillover effect, what matters, 'realists' contend, are the attitudes of member states not the role of supranational institutions. If member states do not want to integrate then they will not do so, and there is not much the Commission can do about it. Five factors can be seen to have underpinned the resurgence of member states' interest in integration in the mid 1980s:[14]
● Expanded EC membership, with Greece joining in 1981 and Portugal and Spain in 1986
● Solution of Britain's budget contribution problem in 1984

● Intensification of pressures from the international political economy, such as competitive threats from hi-tech industries in the USA and Japan
● Failure of trusted regulatory policies to combat economic recession and the turn to right-wing policies of deregulation
● The French Socialist government's abandonment of its reflationary economic policies in 1983 and its move to an austerity programme.

The argument here is that momentum generated at national level through a convergence of preferences favoured European integration. Supranational institutions, such as the Commission under its new President, Jacques Delors, appointed in 1985, Jacques Delors, may have reacted to this convergence and sought to generate 'spillover', but they did not create it. In opposition to neo-functionalists who seek creation of an integrative dynamic at supranational level, 'realists' focus on the impetus national governments give to the process. Keohane and Hoffmann argue that 'successful spillover requires prior programmatic agreements among governments, expressed in an intergovernmental bargain'.[15]

CONTRASTING PERSPECTIVES ON INTEGRATION

Having analysed a number of key terms employed by analysts of European integration it is important to note some contrasts: for example, between intergovernmentalism and supranationalism. Britain has traditionally preferred cooperation through intergovernmental structures rather than integration through supranational arrangements.

Supranationalism implies a central authority with power over member states – the so-called 'Brussels Empire' that alarms Eurosceptics. A federal system would seek to preserve some measure of regional, or sub-supranational, autonomy. The EC already shows signs of federation, albeit a form of 'cooperative federalism' whereby member states and the EC share responsibilities because neither has the authority to tackle the challenges they face on their own.

Explanations of integration are also contrasting. In the 1950s and early 1960s analysts pointed to the dynamic effects of supranational institutions, primarily the Commission, in creating a 'spillover effect' as integration proceeded 'logically' from one sector to another. This view is opposed by those who take a 'realist' view and point to the important role played by member states in determining the speed and direction of integration.

What is clear is that there has been a remarkable process of political and economic integration in the EC since World War Two. The chapters that follow look at this process and at Britain's role in it. The next chapter looks at integration in Europe prior to British accession. Britain was distrustful of supranationalism and stayed out of the EC, thus failing to shape policy priorities that were to prove disadvantageous when it did decide to seek membership.

NOTES

1 W Wallace, *The Dynamics of European Integration* (Pinter/Royal Institute of International Affairs, London, 1990), ch.1.
2 E Haas, 'The Study of Regional Integrations: Reflections on the Joy and Anguish of Pretheorizing', in L Lindberg and S Scheingold (eds) *Regional Integration: Theory and Research* (Harvard University Press, Cambridge, Mass, 1971), p.6.
3 B Laffan, *Integration and Cooperation in Europe* (Routledge, London, 1992), Introduction.
4 Ibid.
5 F Capotori, 'Supranational Organisations', in R Bernhardt (ed) *Encyclopedia of Public International Law,* Instalment 5 (Elsevier, Amsterdam, 1983), 262-8.
6 W Wallace, 'What Price Interdependence? Sovereignty and Interdependence in British Politics', *International Affairs* 62 (1986), p.367.
7 M Burgess, *Federalism and Federation in Western Europe* (Croom Helm, London, 1986)
8 K Wheare, *Federal Government* (Oxford University Press, Oxford, 1963).
9 S Bulmer and W Wessels, *The European Council: Decision-Making in European Politics* (Macmillan, London, 1987).
10 J Loughlin, 'Federalism, Regionalism and European Union', *Politics* 13 (1993), 9-16
11 C Pentland, *International Theory and European Integration,* (Faber and Faber, London, 1973).
12 S George, *Politics and Policy in the European Community,* second edition (Oxford University Press, Oxford, 1991), ch.2.
13 Wallace, op cit, p.7.
14 R Keohane and S Hoffmann, *The New European Community,* (Westview Press, Oxford, 1991), ch.1.
15 R Keohane and S Hoffmann, 'Conclusions: Community Politics and Institutional Change', in Wallace, op cit. p.287.

2 REBUILDING EUROPE

In July 1993 the Tour de France passed the memorial to the thousands killed at Verdun in World War One. On the memorial flew the flags of France and Germany. Between them fluttered the blue flag with the 12 gold stars of the European Community. This scene symbolised the post-war movement towards integration in Europe as a means of undermining nationalistic enmities. It also illustrated the rapprochement between France and Germany which underpins the European Community. At the end of World War Two the French sought to incorporate West Germany into a peaceful European order without risking a restoration of German military power which could once again threaten world peace. Supranational structures of government within which members' sovereignty would be 'pooled' were seen as the answer. First came the ECSC in 1951. Later, in 1957, came the EEC.

EAST VERSUS WEST

After World War Two Europe faced severe economic and political challenges. To the east the Soviet Union consolidated its strength. To the west states looked to their principal ally, the USA, for help. 'Europe had become an object of world politics with the shots being called by the great powers.'[1]

American assistance to Europe came in the form of Marshall Aid, named after Secretary of State George C Marshall who developed the plan to rebuild west European economies. Around $13 billion worth of aid was distributed among west European countries between 1948 and 1952. West Germany was the main beneficiary of Marshall Aid, receiving $4.5 billion. This served to draw it firmly into the Western bloc. By establishing the Organisation for European Economic Cooperation (OEEC) in May 1948, the Americans sought to involve recipient countries in the Marshall Aid distribution process. The British, then the strongest power in Europe, resolutely advocated intergovernmental cooperation in the OEEC rather than institution of supranational structures with powers over member states.

The USA was keen to see the establishment in western Europe of open capitalist economies with liberal-democratic political systems. It made sound commercial sense for the USA to seek to restore the economies of the West because it could then trade with them. It was not only the external threat from the East that perturbed the Americans. There were also strong Communist parties in France and Italy. Restoration of economic prosperity within a capitalist order was seen as a defence against communism in these countries.

On Soviet insistence, Marshall Aid was not accepted in eastern Europe. Both Czechoslovakia and Poland rejected it. This, and the Czech communists' seizure of sole power in February 1948, led Britain, the Benelux countries (Belgium, the Netherlands, and Luxembourg) and France to form the Brussels Treaty organisation in March 1948 whereby they pledged mutual military aid and economic cooperation. Also in March 1948 the three Western occupying powers in Germany – France, Britain and the USA – unified their occupation zones and convened a constitutional assembly which introduced currency reforms that created the Deutschmark (DM). This caused similar steps to be taken in the east of Germany by the fourth occupying power, the Soviet Union. A Soviet attempt to blockade Berlin in the winter of 1948 which, although occupied by the four powers, was surrounded by the Soviet zone of occupation, was breached by allied airlifts.

In April 1949 NATO was established by the Treaty of Washington. This firmly committed the USA to defence of western Europe. In September 1949 the Federal Republic of Germany (FRG) was created. In October 1949 the GDR was established in the east. The division of Germany provided firm evidence of the iron curtain that had fallen across the continent of Europe. The question of what to do about West Germany helped instigate the EC in the 1950s.

INTERGOVERNMENTALISM VERSUS SUPRANATIONALISM

The restoration of nation states after World War Two had dashed the hopes of constitutional federalists who had sought a United States of Europe. In their opinion, only such a dramatic step could transcend the bitterness and divisions that had plagued the continent and generated two world wars in the space of 30 years. Ways forward in a Europe of nation states were unclear.

What was clear was that a basic divide was emerging between Britain on the one hand, and the six countries that were to found the ECSC in 1951 on the other. The British had no intention of participating in a supranational organisation. The Benelux countries had already taken steps towards 'pooling' their sovereignty when, in 1948, they had set up a customs union.

Tensions between supranationalists and intergovernmentalists became apparent at the May 1948 Congress of Europe in The Hague, where over 700 prominent Europeans met to discuss the future of the continent. The outcome of the meeting was creation of the Council of Europe in May 1949. It was located in Strasbourg, on the Franco-German border, in order to symbolise reconciliation between these two countries. Britain's preference for intergovernmentalism prevailed in the Council of Europe: decisions in its Council of Ministers are taken on the basis of unanimity. It has come to be identified with the European Convention on Human Rights (ECHR), signed in November 1950. This, after the atrocities of World War Two, signified a commitment to human rights as binding on sovereign states.

SCHUMAN'S PLAN

A core group of west European countries felt frustrated by Britain's suspicion of supranationalism and, as the Benelux countries had already done in their customs union, sought closer structures of economic integration. It was, and still is, France and (what was then West) Germany that formed the key axis within this supranational integrative project. Plans developed by French foreign minister Robert Schuman were for a common market in coal and steel. The ECSC was an attempt to resolve the question of how to restore German economic prosperity, from which the French would benefit, whilst binding West Germany to a peaceful west European order.

Schuman's plan, proposed on 9 May 1950, led to creation of the ECSC by the Treaty of Paris in April 1951. It created a common market for coal and steel and supranational structures of government to run the community. Schuman's ambitions were not limited simply to coal and steel. As he put it, 'Europe will not be made all at once or according to a single general plan. It will be built through concrete achievements which first create a de facto solidarity'.[2]

The ECSC broke new ground in two ways:
- It laid the foundations for a common market in the basic raw materials needed by an industrial society.
- It was the first European inter-state organisation to show supranational tendencies.

Schuman advocated step-by-step integration. A united Europe was the goal, but it would be achieved through 'spillover' effects (see Chapter 1). A leading ally of Schuman was the Frenchman Jean Monnet who became the first President of the High Authority of the ECSC (the forerunner of the Commission), as well as one of the 'patron saints' of latter-day Euro-enthusiasts.

THE ECSC'S INSTITUTIONS

Four main institutions were created to operate the ECSC. The institutions of the EC developed on this basis:
- The **High Authority** had two main tasks: to make policy proposals and to ensure that member states complied with their obligations. Member states were not allowed to give subsidies and aids to their national coal and steel industries and restrictive practices were outlawed. The High Authority was more than just a bureaucracy, it also had an important political role. Its nine members were not national representatives, they were intended to advance the purposes of European integration
- The **Council of Ministers** was the legislature of the ECSC. There were six members of the Council, with each member state having one representative. As member states were unwilling to lose complete control over key industries, decisions were often made on the basis of unanimity, which meant that decision-making structures were weak. The Council of Ministers nevertheless introduced an important element of intergovernmentalism into the ECSC
- The **Common Assembly** was meant to provide a democratic input into the working of the ECSC. However, members of the Assembly were not directly elected, but were chosen from the ranks of national parliamentarians. They had a purely advisory role and possessed no legislative authority
- A **Court of Justice** was established to settle disputes between member states and the ECSC. When members signed the Treaty of Paris they entered into a binding legal commitment. The role of the Court was to interpret ECSC law in the event of disputes, and thus to

define the parameters of supranational integration. As the remit of EC law has expanded since the 1950s so the Court has become increasingly central to the process of European integration.

Although institution of the ECSC created supranational authority, member states were keen to have the final say in decisions that were taken. They ensured that this happened by making the Council of Ministers the decision-making body of the ECSC. Even today, decision-making power in the EC still largely resides with member states in the Council of Ministers.

TWO STEPS FORWARD, ONE STEP BACK

Hoffmann argues that European integration has tended to falter when it has had to deal with matters of 'high politics', such as foreign affairs and defence, and to prosper when confronted with matters of 'low politics', chiefly welfare.[3] In the early 1950s the morale of federalists was raised by the success of the ECSC, and they looked to build on this success by creating a European Defence Community (EDC). This represented a move into the domain of 'high politics'.

In 1950, when leader of the opposition in Britain, Winston Churchill had called for a unified European army acting in cooperation with the United States and Germany. In office, though, Churchill's Conservative government of 1951 to 1955 was as hostile to supranationalism as had been its Labour predecessor. It refused to join the EDC. The French Left was also opposed to rearmament of Germany within the EDC. The plan was killed off in August 1954 when it was rejected by the French National Assembly. Instead, in the same month, the West European Union (WEU) was established by the six ECSC members, plus Britain, as the west European, intergovernmental, pillar of NATO. The WEU incorporated the vanquished axis powers of Germany and Italy into the collective defence structures of western Europe.

THE ROAD TO ROME

The WEU was a triumph for intergovernmentalists, but federalists were not deterred and returned their attention to economic integration in an attempt to build on the foundations laid by the 1951 Treaty of Paris. What they sought was creation of a common market, like that set up by the Benelux countries in 1948. In June 1955 a conference of foreign ministers was convened in the Italian coastal town of Messina and a committee led by Belgian foreign minister, Paul-Henri Spaak, was asked to look at options for further integration.

The British had observer status at the conference but soon made it clear that they were not interested in supranational integration. The Spaak report was considered by a meeting of ECSC foreign ministers in Venice in May 1956. The outcome was two treaties of Rome signed in March 1957: one established the European Economic Community (EEC) and the other set up the European Atomic Energy Community (Euratom). Thus, there are three founding treaties of the European Communities – the Treaty of Paris (1951) which set up the ECSC and the two Treaties of Rome (1957) which set up the EEC and Euratom.

The EEC has emerged as the predominant organisation. Its founding Treaty was premised on 'an ever closer union of the peoples of Europe'. It abolished trade barriers and customs duties and established a common external tariff, thereby making the EEC a customs union. The EEC was also designed to promote the free movement of people, goods, services and capital within a common market. The member states transferred to the EEC powers to conclude trading agreements with international organisations on their behalf.

Four main institutions, modelled on those set up to run the ECSC, were created to manage the EC:
● The **Commission**, a supranational institution responsible for both policy proposals and implementation
● The **Council of Ministers**, the legislative authority of the EC
● The **Common Assembly** (now known as the European Parliament), which has an advisory role and no legislative authority
● The **Court of Justice**, to umpire matters of dispute relating to EC law.

Chapter 4 investigates the operation of these institutions.

The EEC Treaty also made provision for a Common Agricultural Policy. Agriculture was an obvious candidate for a common policy for three main reasons. Firstly, it would have been illogical to leave this important area of economic activity with member states.[4] Secondly, the EEC and the ECSC addressed a range of industrial issues, such that an agricultural policy was seen as a balance to these concerns. Thirdly, France, with its large agricultural sector, sought protection for its farmers as well as access to markets in other member states. The CAP had three founding principles:

- Common agricultural prices in the EEC
- Common financing (meaning an agricultural budget)
- Community preference over imports.

Much of the EC's Treaty framework is vague and depends heavily on the impetus given to integration by member states. The speed and direction of European integration have always depended heavily on their collective endeavour.

THE BRITISH RESPONSE

Distrustful of supranationalism, the British responded to the EC by instigating EFTA, set up by the Stockholm Convention of July 1959. EFTA was in accord with the British preference for intergovernmentalism. The seven signatories – Denmark, Norway, Sweden, Portugal, Austria, Switzerland and Britain – established a free trade area which brought down barriers to trade between members and sought to keep in touch with EC tariff reductions.

By the early 1960s it had become apparent to the British that EFTA was peripheral to the fast-growing economies of the EC. A powerful trading bloc was emerging on Britain's doorstep from which it was excluded. In the 1960s the EC appeared to be going from success to success as the Common External Tariff was put in place and the CAP established. Britain was forced into a re-evaluation of previous policy and sought membership of the EC. However, French President de Gaulle was distinctly underwhelmed by the prospect of British membership and, in 1963 and 1967, vetoed British accession bids.

THE ORIGINS OF THE EUROPEAN COMMUNITY

A rapid process of European integration was instigated in the 1950s by institution of the ECSC, the EEC and Euratom. What was distinct about these organisations was their supranational structures. Member states were, though, unwilling to cede complete authority to supranational institutions. In consequence, the intergovernmental Council of Ministers was made the legislative authority of the Communities.

Supranational integration failed to break into the domain of 'high politics' following rejection of the EDC in 1954. Economic integration has tended to prove easier for the EC to achieve than political integration. Economic interdependence is readily apparent in post-war Europe, and from the ECSC of 1951 to the single market of 1993 structures to manage that interdependence have been created. In the sphere of 'high politics', countries have been keen to preserve the right to act in accord with their own national interests.

Britain remained aloof from supranational organisations. However, this was not just the product of its distrust of supranationalism. As the US Secretary of State, Dean Acheson, put it in 1960, the British had lost an Empire and were trying to find a role. By the end of the 1950s a basic divide had emerged in Europe between the 'EC 6' and the 'EFTA 7'. The EC has proved to be the magnet to which EFTA countries have been attracted. By 1993 most of the EFTA member states had either joined the EC (Britain, Denmark and Portugal) or were apparently on the verge of doing so (Austria, Sweden and Norway). Of the original EC and EFTA members only the Swiss continued to steer clear of supranational integration.

NOTES

1 J Story (ed), *The New Europe* (Blackwell, Oxford, 1993), p.11.
2 Quoted in N Nugent, *The Government and Politics of the European Community*, second edition (Macmillan, London, 1991), p.35.
3 S Hoffmann, 'Obstinate or Obsolete: The Fate of the Nation State and the Case of Western Europe', *Daedalus* 95 (1966), 862-915.
4 In the 1950s and 1960s agriculture was far more central to economic life than it is today. In 1959, 24 per cent of the EC's population was employed in the agricultural sector. By 1991, this figure had fallen to 6 per cent, and agriculture accounted for less than 3 per cent of EC GDP.

3 BRITAIN JOINS THE CLUB

British policy towards the EC was re-evaluated in the 1960s. Both Macmillan (in 1963) and Wilson (in 1967) pursued membership of the Community, only to be rebuffed by de Gaulle's veto. It was left to Heath to lead Britain into the EC in January 1973. With hindsight it can be argued that Britain stayed out of the Community when it should have joined in the 1950s, and joined when it should have stayed out in the 1970s. Britain spent its first decade of membership arguing about the terms of accession and seeking a budget rebate. After the budget issue had been resolved in June 1984 the British were keen advocates of a single market within which people, goods, services and capital could move freely. Yet neither Thatcher nor Major has been enthusiastic about the implications of the single market. After 20 years of EC membership, Britain has acquired the reputation of an 'awkward partner'.[1]

1960S: BRITAIN SAYS YES, DE GAULLE SAYS NO

It can be argued that British political élites made three fundamental miscalculations about the EC in the 1950s:[2]

● The British government held the view that supranational integration was foredoomed and that the EC's federalising tendencies would soon founder on the rocks of member states' national concerns. The British refused to join the ECSC and the EDC and only sent a senior civil servant to the Messina negotiations in 1955 which led to the Rome Treaties of 1957. Other countries dispatched eminent politicians

● Britain believed that the problems of the post-war era could be met by establishing a free trade area (EFTA), and that supranational integration was unnecessary

● The British under-estimated the obstacles to accession once a distinct course of action had been decided upon. The applications of prime ministers Macmillan and Wilson were both blocked by French President de Gaulle.

De Gaulle's vision was of Europe as a third force between the super-powers of East and West, ideally with him as its leader. He thought Britain would seek to dominate the EC and place it firmly in the American bloc. Britain and America shared a 'globalist' perspective, of which central features were commitment to an open world trading order and rejection of protectionism.

Three broad characteristics of British policy towards the EC in the 1950s should be highlighted:
- Aloofness towards Europe based on a perception, as Churchill put it, that Britain was 'with them' against the greater foe of communism, but not 'of them' in participating in integration
- Opposition to the supranational implications of the EC which were seen as eroding national sovereignty. In Britain a sense of national identity had been strengthened by the experience of World War Two. The sovereignty that had been so keenly defended then was not about to be ceded to supranational institutions in Europe
- Development of an alternative policy focused on the Empire and the 'special relationship' with the USA. Europe was seen as one of three interlocking circles, but as third in the order of priorities.

By the early 1960s the British government was questioning its aloofness towards the EC. The 'special relationship' with the USA had been dented by the Suez crisis of 1956, when the USA had declined to support Britain's military intervention in Egypt. It was beginning to seem that the relationship was more special in British eyes than in American, and that post-war hopes of partnership had been replaced by an economic and military dependence by means of which Britain was consigned to a role of 'increasingly impotent avuncularity'.[3]

Britain was also worried that its close ties with America could be supplanted by links between the USA and the EC. The USA feared that de Gaulle's 'third force' aspirations for Europe would weaken the Western alliance, and hoped Britain would steer the EC in a direction sympathetic to American interests. In July 1962 President Kennedy called for an Atlantic partnership between the USA and the EC, including Britain. He wanted to see an outward-looking and open EC.

In the 1960s the Commonwealth ideal that nations of the former Empire could cooperate on an equal footing took several dents. Divisions emerged between the 'black' and 'white' Commonwealth over, for example, Britain's less than wholehearted denunciation of the South African regime after the Sharpeville massacre of 1961. Conflict also arose between India and Pakistan over the disputed territory of Kashmir, and more generally over the unilateral declaration of independence made by Ian Smith's regime in Rhodesia in 1965.

By the time Harold Wilson became prime minister in 1964, economic concerns impelled the membership bid. EFTA was not proving a success when compared to the dynamic economies of the EC, and Commonwealth trading patterns were changing as Australia and New Zealand looked to markets in the USA and Japan. Wilson had come to office espousing 'the white heat of the scientific revolution' that would modernise the British economy. Larger markets were needed for high technology industries – such as aircraft and computers – but exclusion from the EC meant separation from fast-growing neighbouring economies.

On all usual economic indicators Britain was lagging behind the EC. For example, between 1958 and 1968 real earnings in Britain rose by 38 per cent, compared to 75 per cent in the EC. Fear of isolation is apparent in a memorandum sent by Macmillan to his Foreign Secretary, Selwyn Lloyd, in 1959:

> For the first time since the Napoleonic era the major continental powers are united in a positive economic grouping, with considerable political aspects, which, although not specifically directed against the United Kingdom, may have the effect of excluding us both from European markets and from consultation in European policy.

1973: MEMBERSHIP

In 1969 the political complexion of the two countries at the heart of European integration – France and West Germany – changed in a way advantageous to Britain's membership hopes. In France President de Gaulle resigned and was replaced by Pompidou, who favoured British accession. In West Germany the new Social Democratic government, led by Willy Brandt, was also keen to see enlargement of the EC.

However, prior to the accession of new member states the founder members laid down a budgetary framework for the Community at a heads of government meeting in The Hague in 1969. This was formalised by Treaty in 1970. Construction of the EC's 'own resources' was not to Britain's advantage as it effectively penalised countries with extensive trading links outside the EC. When goods from outside the EC enter a member state they face the EC's common external tariff which, after collection, becomes part of the Community's 'own resources'. Having substantial trading links with non-EC countries, notably those in the Commonwealth, Britain was disadvantaged from the start by this measure. In addition, Britain, with a relatively efficient agricultural sector, has never gained much profit from the main financial activity of the EC, farm price support.

Negotiations on British accession began in June 1970 under Conservative Prime Minister Edward Heath. In July 1971 a White Paper was published. It noted some of the disadvantages of membership:
● It was estimated that food prices would go up by 15 per cent over a six-year period because the CAP contained a system of Community preference which would mean that Britain could no longer shop around on cheaper world food markets
● Increased food prices would contribute to a 3 per cent increase in the cost of living over a six-year period
● British contributions to the EC budget would amount to £300 million a year, making Britain the second largest contributor behind West Germany. British contributions would be high because it had extensive external trading links.

Britain joined the EC on 1 January 1973, along with Denmark and Ireland. (Norway also negotiated accession terms but the Norwegian people rejected membership in a referendum.) Although Prime Minister Heath was pursuing a policy developed by his predecessors, who had come to the conclusion that EC membership was necessary if Britain was not to risk economic and political isolation, he was more than merely a pragmatic European. Indeed, Heath was in the 1970s a keen advocate of membership and is still a convinced Euro-enthusiast. He also of course realised that on pragmatic grounds Britain had little option but to enter the EC and try to shape it from within. On 28 October 1971 MPs voted by 356 to 244 in favour of accession to the Community. The Conservatives were allowed a free vote whilst Labour imposed a three-line whip against accession. In the event 69 Labour MPs voted in favour of joining the Community. Current party leader John Smith was among them.

British accession occurred just as the economies of western Europe were ending their long post-war period of economic growth. Britain could hardly have chosen a less propitious moment to dip a tentative toe into the waters of supranational economic and political integration. Oil price increases soon helped to plunge the British and European economies into recession.

1974-75: RENEGOTIATION AND REFERENDUM

For Harold Wilson Britain's membership of the EC posed something of a dilemma. He had sought accession as Prime Minister in the 1960s, but in Britain's adversarial political system he could not pass up the chance of picking up a stick with which to beat the Conservative government. What Wilson did was oppose the *terms* of accession – as negotiated by Heath – and pledge a future Labour government to renegotiation and a referendum.

After Labour returned to power in February 1974 renegotiation talks were led by Foreign Secretary James Callaghan. Britain gained little through renegotiation that it could not have gained through normal Community channels. Furthermore, the degree of acrimony engendered by the bargaining soured Britain's relations with other members for many years. The House of Commons endorsed the renegotiated terms by 396 votes to 170 in April 1975. Ominously for the Labour government, and despite pro-Community speeches from both Wilson and Callaghan, a special Labour conference on 26 April 1975 voted by 3.7 million to 1.9 million to leave the EC.

The pledge to hold a referendum helped Wilson overcome divisions within the Labour Party. Indeed, it seems likely that this was the referendum's major purpose. During the referendum campaign of 1975 Wilson suspended the convention of collective Cabinet responsibility so that Cabinet ministers could speak according to their consciences. The 'Yes' campaign commanded powerful political assets despite opinion polls at the outset pointing to a 'No' vote. It had strong support from Fleet Street and from powerful business interests which provided a large part of the £1.5 million spent in the quest for an affirmative vote. It also gathered a powerful coalition of centrist politicians, including Heath, Labour's Roy Jenkins and Liberal leader Jeremy Thorpe. By comparison, the 'No' campaign raised just £133,000. It found itself outgunned and was weakened by its disparate character: Tony Benn from the left of the Labour Party formed a decidedly uneasy temporary alliance with right-wing Conservatives such as Enoch Powell. The outcome, on 5 June 1975, was a two to one vote in favour of continued membership on a 64 per cent turnout.[4]

1976-79: CALLAGHAN'S DIFFICULTIES

In April 1976 James Callaghan succeeded Harold Wilson as Prime Minister and inherited a Labour Party divided over EC membership. Labour's rank and file distrusted the EC even though some prominent Labour politicians, such as Roy Jenkins and Shirley Williams, were keen advocates of membership. There were two main areas of concern. First, it was felt that integration into a supranational community would restrict national sovereignty and the freedom of action of a Labour government. Secondly, the EC was seen as a 'capitalist club' with market-based purposes that offered little to working people. Arguments over EC membership were symptomatic of a deeper malaise within the Labour Party that saw the leadership frequently at odds with the membership and culminated in right-wingers splitting to form the Social Democratic Party (SDP) in January 1981.

In February 1975 the Conservatives replaced Edward Heath as leader with Margaret Thatcher. Thatcher had opposed the 1975 referendum describing it, in a phrase that would come back to haunt her in her Euro-sceptical dotage, as a device for demagogues. She argued for a 'Yes' vote on the grounds that Britain needed to foster economic links with the European markets on its doorstep.

Prime minister Callaghan was also a pragmatist and an Atlanticist who held no truck with the lofty rhetoric of European union. He had a poor reputation in EC circles as a result of his dogged pursuit of national interests during the British renegotiation, and failed as premier to ease tensions caused by Britain's entry to the Community.

From March 1977 Callaghan relied on support from the Liberals to sustain his administration. This support was conditional on insertion of a clause introducing proportional representation (PR) as the method of voting in direct elections to the European Parliament. Such a clause was duly inserted into the European Assembly Elections Bill of 1977. However, it provoked a Cabinet revolt and, on a free vote in the House of Commons, was defeated. It also delayed direct elections which, to the irritation of other member states, were put back from 1978 to 1979.

The British Presidency of the EC in the first six months of 1977 did little to enhance Britain's reputation. Callaghan was hamstrung by a Euro-sceptical party and by domestic economic problems. In a letter to the General Secretary of the Labour Party at the start of the British Presidency he outlined three basic principles that informed the Labour government's stance on the EC:

● Maintenance of the authority of EC nation states and national parliaments, with no increase in the powers of the European Parliament

● Emphasis on the necessity for national governments to achieve their own economic, regional and industrial objectives

● Reform of the budget procedure.

Contained within these policy principles is a clear restatement of Britain's suspicion of supranationalism and continued concern over the high level of budget contributions. These concerns were shared by Margaret Thatcher when she became Prime Minister in May 1979. She battled for a budget rebate and opposed extensions of supranational authority, but Britain's reputation as an 'awkward partner' both preceded and has survived her.

British membership of the EC was advocated on pragmatic economic grounds. Britain thought it was joining a common market – an economic organisation – and played down the political consequences of membership. Prime Minister Heath rejected the idea that Britain was joining a putative federation. Pragmatic acceptance of membership means that Britain has tended to judge the EC by utilitarian standards: what does it have to pay and what does it get out of it. Britain was paying a lot in the late 1970s and early 1980s and seemed to be getting little in return. Not surprisingly, enthusiasm for the EC did not run deep.

1979-84: THE BUDGET REBATE

Margaret Thatcher inherited the policy concerns of preceding Labour governments, particularly over the high level of contributions to the EC budget. By the end of the 1970s Britain was the second largest contributor to the budget and was in danger of becoming the largest, paying over £1 billion a year, even though it had the third-lowest GDP per capita of the nine member states.

A series of often acrimonious negotiations was held between 1979 and 1984. Then Commission President, Roy Jenkins, writes in his memoirs of long hours spent discussing the BBQ: the British Budget Question, or as he preferred to put it, the Bloody British Question. He notes how Thatcher made a bad start at the Strasbourg Summit in 1979 when she had a strong case but succeeded in alienating other leaders upon whose support she depended for a deal to be struck. Britain's partners in the Community were unwilling to receive lectures on the issue from Thatcher and were alienated by suggestions that the budget mechanisms were tantamount to theft of British money, particularly as Britain had known the budgetary implications when it had joined the Community.

> Mrs Thatcher had thus performed the considerable task of unneces-
> sarily irritating two big countries (France and Germany), three small
> ones (Netherlands, Denmark and Eire) and the Commission within
> her opening hour of performance at a European Council.[5]

The issue was finally resolved at the Fontainebleau summit in June 1984 when a rebate was agreed amounting to 66 per cent of the difference between Britain's VAT contributions to the budget and its receipts. The scheme was in operation from 1985 onwards, and gen-erated a British rebate of approximately Ecu one billion a year.

This agreement was important as it meant the leaders of the Community could lift their sights from interminable squabbles over the budget and begin to think strategically about the future of the Community. The British government's preferences had been clearly stated in a paper, entitled 'Europe – The Future', circulated at the Fontainebleau summit.[6] The paper called for the attainment by 1990 of a single market within which goods, services, people and capital could move freely. It very clearly reflected the deregulatory zeal which Thatcher brought to domestic politics.

1984-87: TOWARDS THE SINGLE MARKET

In Britain Thatcher had sought to 'roll back the frontiers of the state' and allow free enterprise and market forces to flourish.[7] State struc-tures of almost any kind were anathema. For Thatcherites the EC was a stultifying bureaucracy that could do with a dose of Thatcherite vigour, whether it liked it or not.

In order to secure the single market promoted in the Fontainebleau paper Britain needed allies amongst its EC partners. There were potential allies at both the national and supranational level:

● The two key member states, France and West Germany, were amenable to single market reforms. The French Socialist government elected in 1981 had been forced to abandon its reflationary economic policies in 1983, and the Christian Democrat-led coalition of Chancellor Kohl in West Germany supported creation of a single market

● New Commission President, Jacques Delors, took office in 1985 and seized upon the single market as his 'big idea' to restart integration and shake off the 'Eurosclerosis' of the 1970s and early 1980s. Delors was assisted in his ambitions by the Commissioner responsible for the internal market, former Conservative Cabinet minister Lord Cockfield.

A White Paper prepared by the Commission put forward 300 legislative proposals for the single market. These were later whittled down to a mere 282. The proposals were accepted by heads of government at the Milan summit in June 1985. In the face of objections from the Danes, Greeks and British, an intergovernmental conference was convened to consider reform of the EC's decision-making process to accompany the single market plan.

Whilst Britain was hostile to strengthening Community institutions, France and West Germany asserted that attainment of the single market in fact necessitated increased powers for supranational institutions such as the European Parliament in order to ensure that democratic accountability followed the transfer of authority to the supranational level. The British did not see it that way and thought the single market could be achieved without reform of the EC's institutional structure. The result was a compromise package: the 1986 Single European Act (SEA). This had two main features:

● Establishment of a target date, the end of 1992, for completion of the internal market and attainment of the 'four freedoms': freedom of movement of people, goods, services and capital

● Strengthening of EC institutional structures, with qualified majority voting (QMV) introduced in the Council of Ministers extended to cover ten new policy areas relating to harmonisation measures necessary to achieve the single market. Increased use of QMV ensured swifter decision-making. Unanimity, though, is still required for fiscal policy, the free movement of persons and employees' rights legislation. The European Parliament's role was strengthened by introduction of the 'cooperation procedure' which gives it power to suggest amendments to Community legislation. The Council retain the right to reject amendments (see Chapter 4 for further details).

The White Paper put forward by the Commission identified three kinds of barriers to trade that needed to come down if the single market was to be attained:

- **Physical barriers** (mainly customs and immigration controls). In January 1986 a standardised customs form was introduced to replace the existing 78 as a prelude to their abolition at all internal border controls at the end of 1992
- **Fiscal barriers** Indirect taxes vary in the Community and constitute a barrier to trade. The White Paper proposed harmonisation within two bands: 14-20 per cent for normal goods, and 4-9 per cent for essential goods, such as most foodstuffs
- **Technical barriers** These were the most important as member states had developed their own product standards which differed widely and formed a substantial barrier to free trade.

The British government objected to large parts of the White Paper. With regard to removal of physical barriers, it had long been concerned to prevent free movement of people, fearing the implications for terrorism, drugs trafficking and illegal immigrants. However, in June 1989 a meeting in Palma of EC interior ministers advocated intergovernmental cooperation on this issue. Indeed, a core group of member states had already made significant steps in the direction of free movement of people. On 14 June 1985 West Germany, France and the Benelux countries signed at Schengen, in Luxembourg, an agreement gradually to abolish all frontier controls between them. Subsequently, Italy, Spain and Portugal joined, whilst Greece took observer status. The Schengen Agreement introduces an element of 'variable geometry' into the EC's integrative process as, some member states have decided to seek closer patterns of integration.

The British government was also opposed to fiscal harmonisation. Indeed, in 1988, Thatcher refused to endorse re-appointment of Lord Cockfield who was seen as having 'gone native' in Brussels largely over this issue. Nevertheless, in 1991 and 1992 three meetings of EC economics and finance ministers took important steps towards VAT harmonisation. Even British Chancellor Norman Lamont was obliged to agree that from 1 January 1993 each member state would set only one standard rate of VAT at not less than 15 per cent (the standard rate of VAT in Britain is 17.5 per cent), that all higher rates would thus be abolished, and that only consumer products of a social or cultural nature would be taxed at a lower rate of not less than 5 per cent. For a transitional period, however, zero rates can be maintained.

Possibly most problems were faced in the sphere of technical barriers. Here, they were greater for the Commission than for the British government. Required to eliminate barriers to free trade, the Commission found itself teetering on the edge of the regulatory nightmare of having to define what constitutes particular products so that common standards could exist across the Community. In the event, it got round the problem by using a 1979 ECJ decision over the French liqueur *Cassis de Dijon* to establish the important principle of *mutual recognition*. The original dispute had been between France and West Germany over the level of alcoholic content necessary to a liqueur: by German standards, *Cassis* did not qualify. The ECJ ruled that if a product is legally produced in one member state then it can be legally sold in another, provided that matters like public safety in the importing country are satisfied.

The benefits of a single European market were claimed to be substantial. A 1988 study, *The Costs of Non-Europe*, found that savings to business and commerce through removal of barriers could be in the region of Ecu 200 billion, corresponding to a potential annual growth rate of approximately 5 per cent. The report calculated that within five years of completion the internal market could generate five million new jobs.[8] By the end of 1992 the main legislative phase of the single market programme had been completed with 233 measures in force, of which 194 required national implementing measures. By 1 January 1993, Denmark had implemented 88 per cent of the single market directives to place it top of the table of compliers. Belgium, on the other hand, had enforced only 68 per cent and was at the bottom of the table. The UK had implemented 73 per cent.

From 1 January 1993 people, goods, services and capital were supposed to be able to move freely within the EC. Divisions over the relaxation of controls on the free movement of people have, however, prompted a separate agreement at Schengen by which a core group of member states have attempted to move faster on allowing their nationals free movement.

1987-90: THATCHER'S LAST HURRAH

The final years of Margaret Thatcher's premiership were characterised by an almost incessant battle against spillover effects generated by the SEA. For the French and Germans, who had been key single market allies, adoption of a plan to complete the single market was a new beginning for integration. They sought to consolidate the success of the SEA by promoting integration in other areas. Plans were hatched for economic and monetary union (EMU) and for Community social policies to ensure minimum rights for workers in the wake of the freedoms given to capital by the SEA (for further details on both policy areas see Chapter 5).

Thatcher firmly set herself against the integrative consequences of the SEA. As she languished in the opinion polls in 1990 her perceived anti-Europeanism was seen as an electoral liability and was one of the factors which precipitated the challenge to her leadership. The final straw for her opponents came in November 1990 when her former Chancellor of the Exchequer and Foreign Secretary, Sir Geoffrey Howe, bitterly criticised her leadership style. Howe's speech was the beginning of the end for Thatcher's premiership, although her successor, John Major, was perceived as the inheritor of the Thatcherite mantle, not least by Thatcher herself.

1990-93: MAJOR AND MAASTRICHT

Within the EC John Major has adopted a more emollient tone than his predecessor and has expressed the intention of placing Britain 'at the heart of Europe'. But, in Major's vision of the Community, made manifest by his negotiation of the Maastricht Treaty in December 1991, there are distinct policy continuities with his predecessor:

● An opt-out from the Social Chapter
● The right for the British Parliament to decide whether Britain will enter the third stage of the plan for EMU when a single currency should be introduced
● Promotion of the notion of subsidiarity, which, in the eyes of the British government, is a way of reinforcing national perspectives on Community decision-making
● Advocacy of intergovernmental cooperation rather than supranational integration as the basis of cohesion in foreign, defence and interior policy. Intergovernmental 'pillars' were incorporated into the Maastricht Treaty.

Unconstrained by high office Baroness Thatcher has remarked that she would never have signed the Maastricht Treaty. However, many argue that the Treaty Major negotiated and signed merely reflected policy preferences Thatcher herself had displayed when in office. In addition, Major also reaped the integrative whirlwind Prime Minister Thatcher had helped initiate when she signed the SEA in 1986.

Major's deal at Maastricht temporarily assuaged Tory divisions over Europe and helped lay the foundations for his April 1992 general election victory. A conspicuous feature of the election campaign was lack of debate about Britain's place in the EC. Both Conservative and Labour party managers knew their parties to be deeply divided on the issue, and tacitly conspired to keep silent about it. Euro-sceptics were thus not entirely unjustified in later complaining that the British people had *not* in fact endorsed Maastricht at the 1992 general election, and that they should therefore be allowed a referendum on the issue.

Safely returned to government, Conservative divisions over Europe could no longer be hidden. A small and determined band of Euro-sceptics frequently defied the government by calling for a referendum on Maastricht and trying to block passage of the Maastricht Bill through the House of Commons. The Euro-sceptics' rebellion culminated in July 1993 when they contributed to a government defeat on incorporation of the Social Chapter into the Maastricht Treaty (from which Major had famously opted-out). Major's response was to 'go nuclear' and turn the issue of Maastricht into one of confidence in the government. In the face of near-certain defeat in a general election and the return of a pro-European Labour government, the Tory rebels returned to the party fold.

BRITISH PRAGMATISM IN EUROPE

It is pragmatism, not idealism, that has shaped Britain's relations with the EC. Britain was distrustful, and to some extent still is, of supra-nationalism. Policy has tended to be continuous between Labour and Conservative governments. For all the distinctiveness of her style, Margaret Thatcher in fact pursued similar EC polices to both her Labour predecessor James Callaghan and her Conservative successor John Major.

British EC membership was advocated to avoid political and economic isolation. It was, in effect, a recognition of Britain's reduced status in world affairs as it declined from superpower status to that of a middle-ranking regional power. By not joining in the 1950s or 1960s established in important areas, such as agriculture and the budget, were not to Britain's advantage. When it did join was soon involved in acrimonious arguments over matters like the budget contribution.

The result of British pragmatism has often been isolation in Community circles and apparent cultivation of a reputation for awkwardness. In the 1980s Britain embraced the notion of a single European market with gusto as it mirrored domestic policy preferences. The British Conservative government, though, was soon to find itself at odds with other Community members over the 'spillover' consequences of the SEA. The issue of sovereignty – or where power lies – became central to British debate. The next chapter investigates Community institutions and assesses how power actually is distributed within the EC.

NOTES

1 S George, *An Awkward Partner: Britain in the European Community* (Oxford University Press, Oxford, 1989).
2 M Beloff, *The Intellectual in Politics, and Other Essays* (Weidenfeld and Nicolson, London, 1970).
3 G Edwards, 'Britain and Europe', in Story, op cit, ch.8.
4 On the referendum see A King, *Britain Says Yes: The 1975 Referendum on the Common Market* (American Enterprise Institute, Washington, DC, 1977), and D Butler and U Kitzinger, *The 1975 Referendum* (Macmillan, London, 1976).
5 R Jenkins, *A Life at the Centre* (Macmillan, London, 1991), p.495.
6 HM Government, 'Europe: The Future', *Journal of Common Market Studies* 23 (1984), 74-81.
7 A Gamble, *The Free Economy and the Strong State: The Politics of Thatcherism* (Macmillan, London, 1988).
8 P Cecchini, *1992: The Benefits of a Single Market* (Gower, Aldershot, 1988).

4 INSTITUTIONS OF THE EUROPEAN COMMUNITY

EC institutions hold powers that shape the lives of citizens of the European Union (created by the Maastricht Treaty). This chapter investigates EC decision-making processes. Community institutions can appear rather dull and their procedures arcane, but this should not disguise the intensely political and, at times, controversial nature of their roles and responsibilities.

THE BRUSSELS EMPIRE?

There are five main EC institutions:
- **The Commission**, which neo-functionalist theorists saw as a potential driving force of integration and which, particularly under the Presidency of Jacques Delors since 1985, has entered the political demonology of Euro-sceptics
- **The Council of Ministers**, the legislative authority of the Community
- **The European Parliament**, the only Community institution which is directly elected
- **The European Court of Justice**, which interprets the growing body of Community law
- **The European Council**, convened at summit meetings of heads of government.

A characteristic of the EC's political system is its amalgam of intergovernmentalism and supranationalism. Because they have been unwilling to cede too much authority to supranational institutions, such as the European Parliament and the Commission, member states have preserved an important input into EC decision-making structures through intergovernmental forums, such as the Council of Ministers and the European Council.

In the 1980s and 1990s the resurgence of integration has strengthened supranationalism. However, many argue that a 'democratic deficit' remains: EC institutions seem distant from ordinary people and are rarely understood by them. It would seem that democracy and accountability may have been casualties in the EC's political system as powers ceded to the Community have tended to fall in a grey area between the control of democratic institutions at either national or supranational level.

THE COMMISSION

A new Commission is appointed every four years. The most recent set of officials took office on 1 January 1993, headed by President Jacques Delors. The Commission has two main roles. First, it makes policy proposals to the Council of Ministers. Secondly, it is responsible for implementation of policies once they have been agreed by the Council of Ministers.

However, the Commission is more than simply the EC's bureaucracy. It also plays an important political role. It may not have fulfilled the aspirations of neo-functionalists who, in the 1950s, saw it as leading the way towards a United States of Europe. Nevertheless, in the 1980s, it was instrumental in the resurgence of integration. It was a Commission White Paper which contained the plans for the single market, and the Commission also pushed hard for EMU and the social dimension.[1]

There are 17 Commissioners: two each from the five largest countries (Britain, France, Germany, Italy and Spain) and one from each of the rest (Table 4.1, opposite). Article 158 of the Treaty of Rome states that: 'The members of the Commission shall be appointed by common accord of the Governments of the member states'. Their appointment is actually determined by heads of government of the member states. Countries which can appoint two Commissioners tend to appoint one from each of the two leading political parties. The current British Commissioners are former Conservative Cabinet minister, Sir Leon Brittan, and former Labour Secretary of State for Scotland, Bruce Millan. The President of the Commission is responsible for allocation of portfolios, although larger and more powerful member states expect to see their Commissioners in prestigious posts. Only one of the Commissioners appointed in 1993, Christiane Scrivener from France, is a woman. In the light of the EC's commitment, reaffirmed at Maastricht, to equal opportunities, this is both ironic and disappointing.

Table 4.1 Commission of the European Communities, 1993-94[1]

Jacques Delors (France)	President
Henning Christopherson (Denmark)	Economic, monetary and financial affairs
Manuel Marin (Spain)	Cooperation and development
Martin Bangemann (Germany)	Industrial policy
Sir Leon Brittan (Britain)	External economic affairs
Abel Matutes (Portugal)	Energy, transport
Peter Schmidhuber (Germany)	Budgets
Christiane Scrivener (France)	Customs, taxation and consumer policy
Bruce Millan (Britain)	Regional policy
Karel van Miert (Belgium)	Competition
Hans van den Broek (Netherlands)	External political relations
Joao de Deus Pinheiro (Portugal)	Relations with the European Parliament
Padraig Flynn (Ireland)	Social affairs
Antonio Ruberti (Italy)	Science, research and development
René Steichen (Luxembourg)	Agriculture
Ioannis Paleokrassas (Greece)	Environment, fisheries
Raniero Vanni d'Archirafi (Italy)	Internal market

1 On ratification of the Maastricht Treaty the Commission will hold office for two years, after which appointment of a new Commission will coincide with elections to the European Parliament (held every five years). Each new Commission will then have to receive the assent of the European Parliament before it can take office.

Article 153 of the Treaty of Rome states that Commissioners should be independent of their national governments in the conduct of their duties, although it is no bad thing if they keep in touch with domestic political developments as a means of assessing their potential impact on Community decision-making. There have been many disputes between Commissioners and the national governments which appointed them. The case of Lord Cockfield, Internal Market Commissioner between 1985 and 1989, is only one of the more celebrated examples of this (see Chapter 3).

The Commission has around 15 000 permanent members of staff, with several thousand others used on a freelance or expert basis. The notion of a 'Brussels Empire' administered by a vast, faceless Commission is rendered rather absurd when its size is compared with that of national bureaucracies. The Commission employs fewer people than the French Ministry of Culture and the British Lord Chancellor's

Department, neither of which is a major department of state. It is smaller than the governments of cities like Amsterdam and Madrid.

The Commission is divided into 23 Directorates General, each of which covers a specific policy area (Table 4.2). DG IX (personnel and administration) is the largest, employing around 2500 people. Next comes DG XII (science, research and development), employing around 1900 people. DG VI (agriculture) is the third largest with over 800 officials.

Table 4.2 Principal administrative units in the Commission, 1993

Secretariat General
Legal Service
Spokesman's Service
Consumer Policy Service
Task Force 'Human Resources, Education, Training and Youth'
Translation Service
Joint Interpretation and Conference Service
Statistical Office

DG I	External relations
DG II	Economic and financial affairs
DG III	Internal market and industrial affairs
DG IV	Competition
DG V	Employment, industrial relationships and social affairs
DG VI	Agriculture
DG VII	Transport
DG VIII	Development
DG IX	Personnel and administration
DG X	Information, communication and culture
DG XI	Environment, nuclear safety and civil protection
DG XII	Science, research and development
DG XIII	Telecommunications, information industries and innovation
DG XIV	Fisheries
DG XV	Financial institutions and company law
DG XVI	Regional policies
DG XVII	Energy
DG XVIII	Credit and investment
DG XIX	Budgets
DG XX	Financial control
DG XXI	Customs union and indirect taxation
DG XXII	Coordination of structural policies
DG XXIII	Enterprises' policy, distributive trades, tourism & social economy

Euratom Supply Agency
Security Office

Nugent outlines six main areas of Commission activity:[2]
- **Initiator and proposer of policies** The Commission makes around 700 to 800 policy proposals a year to the Council of Ministers. By the end of 1992 233 policy proposals relating to the single market had been accepted by the Council of Ministers
- **Executive functions** The Commission has rule-making powers for aspects of technical and administrative law not covered by the Treaties. It makes around 4000 to 5000 of these rules a year. A second executive function is its responsibility for management of Community finances (Ecu 69 billion in 1993). The Commission also supervises front-line policy implementation. An important constraint on the Commission is its small size compared to national bureaucracies which means that it cannot act alone to ensure compliance with EC policies and relies heavily on cooperation with national bureaucracies. Some countries have proved better than others at implementing their legal obligations. A Commission report in November 1990 noted only 40 per cent implementation of single market directives in Italy, compared with 88 per cent in Denmark and 84 per cent in Britain. The Commission can issue *regulations* which are binding in their entirety and directly applicable to all member states. A *directive* can be issued which is binding as to the results to be achieved, but the form and method of implementation are left up to the member states. *Recommendations* and *opinions* are also issued but they are not binding on the member states
- **Guardian of the legal framework** The Commission ensures that the Treaties and Community law are respected. If it spots infringement it issues a letter of formal notice. Around 6000 of these are issued every year. This usually suffices, but if compliance does still not occur then the Commission can deliver a reasoned opinion, of which around 200 are issued each year. The final recourse is to refer the case to the ECJ. About 100 cases are referred to the Court each year. The Court has powers to fine offending parties. In April 1986 a price-fixing cartel led by Montedison, ICI, Shell and Hoechst was fined Ecu 55 million (£35 million) by the ECJ. Article 143 of the Maastricht Treaty gives the Court power to impose fines on member states which do not comply with their Treaty obligations
- **External representative** In some policy areas, such as the GATT world trade talks, member states have ceded authority to the Community to act as their representative
- **Mediator and conciliator** The Commission can play a role as 'honest broker' in disputes between Community institutions and member states

● **Conscience of the Community** British former Commissioner Christopher Tugenhadt noted that the Commission seeks: 'to represent the general interest in the welter of national ones and to point the way ahead'.

THE COUNCIL OF MINISTERS

The Council of Ministers is the legislative authority of the EC. There are 12 members of the Council, one from each member state. In reality there is not a Council of Ministers but a series of Councils depending on which policy area is being discussed. The three areas covered most frequently by Council meetings are foreign affairs (known as the General Council), economics and finance (ECOFIN) and agriculture.

As the Council of Ministers is the legislative authority of the Community its decision-making procedures are very important. In July 1965 French President de Gaulle asserted the right of national veto over what he saw as a worrying trend towards supranationalism through extended use of majority voting in the Council. In January 1966 agreement was reached between the French and other Community members in the *Luxembourg Accord* which, although not having legal effect, recognised national vetoes where 'vital interests' were threatened. For a long time afterwards majority voting was used only for budgetary and administrative matters. Use of national vetoes reinforced intergovernmentalism with its attendant emphasis on unanimity, and was instrumental in the Eurosclerosis of the 1970s when the Community appeared incapable of acting.

A shift towards QMV accompanied the resurgence of integration in the 1980s. Article 100A of the SEA introduced a new legislative procedure – the cooperation procedure – for ten policy areas, largely related to completion of the single market. Qualified majorities are based on a system of weighted votes (Table 4.3, opposite).

Qualified majority voting means that one country alone cannot block a piece of legislation covered by majority voting procedures. The minimum requirement is a coalition of two big states and one small one. In the 1980s increased use of QMV was seen as a way of unblocking the Community's decision-making procedures and ensuring attainment of the single market. The most important feature of the new procedures quickened the Community's decision-making processes.

Before the SEA a directive creating technical norms or standards took 31 months in the Council. With the introduction of QMV it took 13.

Table 4.3 Distribution of weighted votes in the Council of Ministers, 1993

Britain, France, Germany, Italy	10 votes
Spain	8 votes
Belgium, Greece, the Netherlands, Portugal	5 votes
Denmark, Ireland	3 votes
Luxembourg	2 votes
Total	76 votes
Qualified majority	**54 votes**

The country holding the Presidency of the Community, which changes every six months, takes the chair in the Council of Ministers. The office of President is held in turn by each member state for a period of six months, in the following order:

● For a first cycle of six years beginning in January 1987: Belgium, Denmark, Germany, Greece, Spain, France, Ireland, Italy, Luxembourg, Netherlands, Portugal, United Kingdom

● For the following cycle of six years beginning in January 1993: Denmark, Belgium, Greece, Germany, France, Spain, Ireland, Netherlands, Luxembourg, United Kingdom, Portugal.

The most recent British Presidency, held during the final six months of 1992, saw two meetings of heads of government in the European Council, at Birmingham and Edinburgh, as well as 42 meetings of the Council of Ministers, usually in Brussels. Britain took the opportunity to prioritise aspects of its vision of the Community. Included in its list were completion of the single market, promotion of the principle of subsidiarity, pursuit of a breakthrough in the GATT talks, and preparation of the ground for Community enlargement.[3] In the space of only six months the Presidency cannot determine the Community's agenda and must be sensitive to the opinions of member states, particularly that which last held the Presidency and that which will hold it next. In effect, there is therefore a *troika* of the past, current and future Presidencies.[4]

Before Commission proposals go to the Council of Ministers they are considered by the Committee of Permanent Representatives (COREPER). COREPER is comprised of member states' diplomatic representatives in the Community who seek to oil the wheels of decision making. In many cases preliminary agreements are reached in COREPER and the Council of Ministers acts as a rubber stamp. The Council of Ministers is also serviced by a General Secretariat employing over 2000 people.

The cooperation procedure, introduced by the SEA, extended the range of QMV and thereby strengthened supranationalism in key areas related to the single market. The cooperation procedure also gave increased powers to the European Parliament which saw its powers further strengthened by the Maastricht Treaty.

THE EUROPEAN PARLIAMENT

There are 518 members of the European Parliament which, since 1979, has been directly elected. In the 1980s and 1990s the Parliament has seen its powers strengthened and, emboldened by a sense of democratic legitimacy bestowed by direct election, has tried to flex its muscles in the Community. Direct elections have taken place in 1979, 1984 and 1989.

The next elections to the European Parliament will be held in June 1994. Then the Parliament will be expanded to 567 members, and the number of British MEPs will be increased from 81 to 87. The change is a result of German reunification, which necessitated more German MEPs and, in a deal struck at the 1992 Edinburgh Summit, balancing increases for other countries. Pressure continues to be put on Britain to align itself with its 11 EC partners by introducing a system of PR for elections to the European Parliament and thereby realise commitments in EC Treaties to a common electoral system. Whether current Italian moves away from PR for national elections will serve to abate this pressure is unclear.

European elections have not yet captured the imagination of EC citizens. Turnout tends to be lower for European than for national elections (Table 4.4). It has been particularly low in Britain. Furthermore, European elections are still essentially domestic contests, and are dominated by national issues (notably when they are held at the same time as national elections). Nevertheless, turnout across the Community has been higher, on average, than in the USA for national elections.

Table 4.4 Turnout in EC states for elections to the European Parliament, 1979-89

	Year	Turnout
Belgium	1979	91.4
	1984	92.2
	1989	90.7
Denmark	1979	47.8
	1984	52.4
	1989	46.2
France	1979	60.7
	1984	56.7
	1989	48.7
Germany	1979	65.7
	1984	56.8
	1989	62.3
Greece	1981	78.6
	1984	77.2
	1989	79.9
Ireland	1979	63.6
	1984	47.6
	1989	68.3
Italy	1979	84.9
	1984	83.4
	1989	81.0
Luxembourg	1979	88.9
	1984	88.8
	1989	87.4
Netherlands	1979	58.1
	1984	50.6
	1989	47.2
Portugal	1987	72.4
	1989	51.2
Spain	1987	68.9
	1989	54.6
UK	1979	32.3
	1984	32.6
	1989	36.2
EC Total	**1979**	**62.4**
	1984	**59.0**
	1989	**57.2**

Source F Jacobs, R Corbett and M Shackleton, *The European Parliament* (Longman, London, 1992), p.26

Political parties within the EC are increasingly coalescing in transnational groupings. Article 138A of the Maastricht Treaty notes the important role that transnational political parties can play in the integrative process: 'Political parties at European level are important as a factor for integration within the Union. They contribute to forming a European awareness and to expressing the political will of the citizens of the Union'. After the 1989 elections the Socialists were the largest party grouping in the European Parliament.

Table 4.5 Political groups in the European Parliament, 1989

Party	MEPs
Socialists	180
European People's Party	162
Liberals, Democrats and Reformists	45
United European Left	28
Greens	28
European Democratic Alliance	21
Rainbow	15
Technical Group of the European Right	14
Left Unity	13
Non-attached	12
Total	**518**

Source Ibid, p.60

The Labour Party, which is a member of the Socialist Group, emerged as the largest British party after the 1989 elections with 45 of the 81 British MEPs. The 32 Conservative MEPs were members, along with Fianna Fail from Ireland and the Gaullist RPR from France, of the European Democratic Alliance. However, they have since affiliated to – but are not yet full members of – the grouping of Christian Democratic parties, the avowedly federalist European People's Party (EPP). The EPP sees itself as an embryonic political party in its own right and has its own federalist programme. Some snippets from its 1989 manifesto – *On the People's Side* – make interesting reading:

> Our goal is the United States of Europe... The EPP sees it as its historical duty to push forward with the unification of Europe and to bring the process to its conclusion... to a political union, to a socially responsible economic and monetary union and to a security union.

By contrast, the Conservative manifesto for the 1989 European elections opposed the vision of economic and monetary union outlined in the Delors Report of 1989 as well as the social charter, abolition of frontier controls and harmonisation of VAT rates. The campaign run by the party was marked by its negative attitude towards Brussels.

One feature of the European Parliament's deliberations is the number of sites on which they take place: the multi-site problem. The Parliament does most of its work in committees which usually meet in Brussels, although every month for one week, except during August, plenary sessions are held in Strasbourg, whilst the Secretariat is based in Luxembourg. National interests prevent a more rational arrangement from being reached.

European Parliament powers were increased in the 1980s. Prior to ratification of the SEA the Parliament only had the right to be *consulted* on legislation. By a two-thirds majority it could vote to sack the Commission and reject the budget. In addition, by the Treaty of 1970 which established the EC's budgetary framework, the Parliament was made joint budgetary authority, alongside the Council of Ministers. The SEA's *cooperation procedure* allowed Parliament a second reading of proposed legislation in specified areas, and the right to suggest amendments (which are, however, not binding on the Council of Ministers). The SEA also gave the European Parliament power of assent over new members of the Community.

The Maastricht Treaty gives the Parliament powers of *co-decision*, tilting the balance of power in the Community towards supranationalism. If, within the cooperation procedure, the Council does not approve a Commission proposal then it will pass to a new 'conciliation committee' on which the Council of Ministers and Parliament will be equally represented. They may agree a joint text which must then be approved by QMV on the Council and by simple majority in Parliament. If the conciliation committee cannot agree, then Parliament will have the right to reject the Commission's proposal by absolute majority.

This new procedure will give the Parliament power of veto in major sectors including single market legislation, consumer protection, health, education and environmental programmes. Maastricht also gives the Parliament power of assent over appointment of the Commission and allows it to request the Commission to submit any proposal when it decides, by an absolute majority, that new legislation is required. Whether the Parliament will have the power to initiate legislation depends on interpretation of the word 'request'.

THE COURT OF JUSTICE

The shift towards supranationalism in the 1980s and 1990s has placed increased strain on the Court of Justice which has the job of interpreting Community law. The Court, based in Luxembourg, consists of 13 judges: one from each member state, plus one extra to ensure that majority verdicts can be reached. Judges are appointed by agreement of member states for a period of six years, with partial replacement every three years. Six change after three years, and the other seven after another three years. There are six advocates general who assist the judges by analysing the arguments of parties in dispute.

As the remit of the EC has expanded so too has the workload of the ECJ. In order to ease the burden Article 168A of the SEA set up a Court of First Instance which has power to hear and determine on points of law only, with a right of appeal to the Court of Justice. The Court of First Instance is not competent to hear cases brought by member states or Community institutions. The distinguishing feature of EC law is that it overrides national law, this principle being confirmed by the landmark judgment of July 1964 in Costa vs ENEL. In English law it was confirmed in 1974 by Aero Zipp Fasteners vs YKK Fasteners (UK) Ltd. In making the judgment, Mr Justice Graham noted that, 'This [European Communities] Act to put it very shortly enacted that relevant Common Market Law should be applied in this country and should, where there is a conflict, override English law'. Nicoll and Salmon note that:

> The principle is a legal and political milestone and is at the heart of the continuing political controversy over the status of the United Kingdom Parliament, which in the nineteenth century, but not consistently earlier, was held to be 'sovereign' in the sense that its powers were unlimited and incapable of being curbed.[5]

THE EUROPEAN COUNCIL

The European Council is a meeting of EC heads of government. It was institutionalised in Paris in 1974 and formalised by the SEA in 1986. It meets twice a year, though extra meetings can be held in the event of exceptional circumstances, and always convenes in the country holding the Presidency of the Community. When Britain held the Presidency in the last six months of 1992 the European Council met twice. There was a special meeting in Birmingham (16 October), ostensibly to discuss the implications of 'Black Wednesday' when sterling was driven out of the ERM, and a main meeting in Edinburgh (11-12 December). Article D of the Maastricht Treaty outlines the role of the European Council: 'The European Council shall provide the Union with the necessary impetus for its development and shall define the general political guidelines thereof'.

The European Council served as an important vehicle for the 'preference convergence' that underpinned the resurgence of integration in the 1980s. This can be illustrated by a survey of decisions made at key European Council meetings in the 1980s and 1990s (Table 4.6).

Table 4.6 Key European Council meetings, 1984-92

Fontainebleau (June 1984)	British budget rebate agreed
Milan (June 1985)	Commission's White Paper on completing the single market adopted
London (December 1986)	Doubling of EC regional development funds agreed
Hanover (June 1988)	Delors committee established to examine prospects for economic and monetary union (EMU)
Madrid (June 1989)	Stage One of EMU set to begin on 1 July 1990
Strasbourg (December 1989)	Social Charter agreed; intergovernmental conference (IGC) on EMU established
Dublin (June 1990)	IGC on Political Union agreed
Rome (October 1990)	Stage Two of EMU set begin on 1 January 1994; IGCs on EMU and Political Union opened
Maastricht (December 1991)	Treaty on European Union agreed
Edinburgh (December 1992)	Budget framework to 2000 agreed; 'Cohesion Fund' of Ecu 14.5 billion set up for poorer member states

In the 1980s and 1990s international summitry has been a key feature of world politics. The European variant – the European Council – has been the scene of many landmark decisions in recent Community history. The pace of Community development is strongly influenced by decisions taken by the European Council, which is the dominant political forum within the EC.

A DEMOCRATIC DEFICIT?

The process of political integration outlined in Chapter 1 suggests that attitudinal integration should be a characteristic of European political integration as citizens of the European Union begin to iden- tify with the supranational institutions that exercise authority over them. However, perhaps not surprisingly in a Community of 350 mil- lion people, these institutions can in fact appear distant. This problem of distance is compounded by a relative absence of clear patterns of democratic accountability. One of the central reasons for this is that the EC's political system is an amalgam of both supranational and intergovernmental elements. Neither level is able to exert clear democratic authority over Community activities when common poli- cies have been established.

Decision-making authority has tended to reside in intergovernmental institutions such as the Council of Ministers and the European Council. Both institutions contain people whose chief responsibilities lie at the national level. Although the policy remit of the EC has expanded, decision-making authority continues to reside with national ministers who are reluctant to be held to account at the European level. This lack of accountability is reinforced by the fact that the Council of Ministers, unlike legislative authorities in all EC member states, meets in secret.

Commissioners are appointed and not elected, although the Europ- ean Parliament, the only directly elected institution, will be given power of assent over the next Commission that takes office in January 1995. The Commission is also extremely open to organised interests. Due to its small size it relies on the kind of information, expertise and political support which interest groups can provide. Some very close relationships have been forged, such as that between DG VI (Agriculture) and the Committee of Professional Agricultural Organisations (COPA).

By 1992 there were over 500 'Eurogroups' seeking to exert pressure on Community policy making. Of these around 50 per cent repre- sented industrial interests, 25 per cent the agricultural and food lob- bies and only 5 per cent were active on behalf of trade unions. Mitchell argues that 'if one is concerned about the nature of the democratic deficit it is also necessary to be aware of the nature of the relationships which are filling the gap'.[6]

The European Parliament's powers are increasing, with co-decision-making introduced by the Maastricht Treaty for some policy areas. It is described as a toothless organisation but its powers exceed those of many national parliaments. Intergovernmentalists, such as the British, fear that a strengthened European Parliament diminishes national parliaments. The German government, on the other hand, is keen to see a much greater extension of the European Parliament's powers than was actually agreed at Maastricht. It argues that democratic structures need to follow the reallocation of powers to Community level.

Lord Plumb, leader of the British Conservatives in the European Parliament, has argued that national parliaments and the European Parliament should be partners, not rivals. Where common policies exist then a Community Parliament would appear to be the most effective way to scrutinise the activities of politicians and officials who wield power at Community level. Shirley Williams suggests that one way to close the 'democratic deficit' would be to create committees on Community affairs in all member states on which MEPs and national parliamentarians could serve together.[7]

The EC is accumulating an increasingly wide range of powers and responsibilities. If member states wish the Community to reflect the liberal democratic political systems they favour then should not democracy and accountability be the watchwords of builders of the Community? Close calls in the French and Danish referenda of 1992 and 1993 would seem to indicate that the political and economic élites that drive EC integration are proceeding too quickly. Citizens of the new European Union are concerned that those who hold power at Community level should not reside in remote institutions.

NOTES

1 P Ludlow, 'The European Commission', in Keohane and Hoffmann, op cit. ch.3
2 Nugent, op cit, ch.3.
3 Foreign and Commonwealth Office, *UK Presidency of the European Communities, July-December 1992* (HMSO, London, 1993).
4 For contrasting views on the UK Presidency see P Ludlow, 'The UK Presidency: A View from Brussels', and T Garel Jones, 'The UK Presidency: An Inside View' both in *Journal of Common Market Studies* 31 (1993), 246-67.
5 W Nicoll and T Salmon, *Understanding the European Communities* (Philip Allan, London, 1990), p.79.
6 D Mitchell, 'Interest Groups and Democratic Deficit' *Europe Access* 2 (April 1993), 14-17.
7 S Williams, 'Sovereignty and Accountability in the European Community', in Keohane and Hoffmann, op cit, ch.5.

5 MAASTRICHT: BLUEPRINT FOR A FEDERAL EUROPE?

Maastricht is a pleasant, rather quiet town in the southern Dutch province of Limburg. It was forced into prominence by the European summit of December 1991 which agreed the Maastricht Treaty.[1] As a city, Maastricht embodies aspects of European integration which may not be apparent to people living in Britain. It is very close to Belgium and Germany, and national borders around it have become meaningless as people cross them on a daily basis for a whole range of activities such as work, education and shopping. A single currency would greatly ease the lives of these people. However, events in August 1993 have made plans for economic and monetary union set out in the Treaty appear unattainable within the timetable envisaged. Consequently, the Maastricht Treaty may not be as integrationist as was once thought. ·

ECONOMIC AND MONETARY UNION

The Treaty of Rome of 1957 recognised the need for coordination of economic policies. Title Two called for 'progressively approximating the economic policies of member states'. A Monetary Committee was established to seek monetary policy coordination, although there was no clear intention to set up a currency bloc in Europe. The post-war international economic order was centred around the Bretton Woods agreement of 1944 which established the US dollar as the bulwark of the Western economic system.

Within the EC the basic structures of the Common Market had been set in place by the late 1960s and heads of government, meeting in The Hague in 1969, decided to take steps to form an EMU to protect the CAP. As the setting of common agricultural prices depended on currency stability, instability would threaten its basis. The heads of government commissioned Pierre Werner, Luxembourg's Prime Minister, to bring forward a plan for EMU. He proposed three stages culminating in an irrevocable fixing of exchange rates and free circulation of people, goods, services, and capital. However, Werner's plan was undermined by events in the 1970s when dollar instability created by the burgeoning US budget deficit was compounded by the 1973 oil crisis and the failure of EC governments to agree a coordinated economic and political response.

FRANCE AND GERMANY RELAUNCH EMU

The French and German governments remained convinced of the merits of further economic integration. In 1978 the Bremen summit established the European Monetary System (EMS) and its Exchange Rate Mechanism (ERM), with the Ecu as a parallel unit of exchange and forerunner of a single currency. The EMS aims to formalise economic cooperation between the member states leading to eventual convergence. The Ecu is based on a 'basket' of EC currencies and is related to the economic strength of member states. Each national currency is valued in relation to the Ecu and, thus, to all other EC currencies with central rates of exchange.

These Ecu rates of exchange form the basis of the ERM which seeks to establish a zone of currency stability within the EC. The ERM fixes national currencies within narrow margins of fluctuation in relation to the Ecu. In 1978 the margin of fluctuation was set at 2.25 per cent, except for the lira which was allowed to operate within wider margins of 6 per cent. The British joined the EMS in 1979, thus making sterling one of the component currencies of the Ecu, but did not join the ERM until October 1990.

Participating member states, as well as powerful business and industrial interests saw three main merits of EMU:
● It would reduce transaction costs generated by currency exchange. In the mid 1980s if an individual with £100 travelled through the 12 EC member states spending no money but changing it at border crossings, he or she would return home with just £53
● It would reduce the uncertainty caused by exchange rate fluctuations which undermine the ability of business to plan ahead
● It would coordinate EC economies and thereby help to create the world's most powerful trading bloc.

EMU implies a single currency, coordination of national economic policies with eventual convergence, and mechanisms for interregional exchange to compensate poorer economies of the Community. Swann likens the position of poorer regions in an EC EMU to that of Northern Ireland now within the United Kingdom. Northern Ireland is the poorest region of the UK but is restricted by an EMU within the UK from taking certain steps – such as devaluing its currency – to improve its competitiveness. Instead, Northern Ireland has to rely on regional aid.[2]

The SEA, from which EMU was perceived as a 'spillover', could be passed off as a largely technical measure designed to bring down barriers to trade without great implications for national sovereignty. EMU cannot be passed off in this way. Control of economic policies and the currency go right to the heart of national sovereignty. As Keynes said, 'Whoever controls the currency, controls the government'. Advocates of European integration contend that economic sovereignty is a chimera in the modern era of economic interdependence and that member states can only exercise effective economic sovereignty as part of an economic union.

After German reunification in November 1989 the French were keen to hasten movement towards EMU in order to subsume potential German economic domination in a form of collective economic management. There were however doubts in Germany as many thought the foundations of German economic success – an independent Bundesbank committed to price stability – could be put at risk by participation in EMU. An opinion poll in April 1993 showed that 60 per cent of Germans were against giving up the Deutschmark with only 29 per cent favouring a single European currency. The driving forces behind the proposal were Paris and the Commission with support from Italy, Belgium and Spain. Germany's main reason for agreeing to participate was political: commitment to EMU was a way of showing continued faith in European integration.

THE EMU PLAN

In June 1988 the European Council set up a Committee for the Study of Economic and Monetary Union, chaired by Commission President Delors. Its report, submitted in April 1989, put forward a three-stage plan for EMU.[3] This formed the basis of the timetable agreed at Maastricht. The Strasbourg summit in December 1989 agreed to set up an IGC to consider Treaty revisions necessary for EMU. The Maastricht Treaty Sets out a timetable for EMU. It is supposed to be achieved by the end of this century at the latest.

The three stages on the path to EMU are as follows:

- **Stage One** All countries to enter the ERM. The Madrid summit in June 1989 set 1 July 1990 as the target date for ERM entry. Sterling finally joined on 8 October 1990 with a fluctuation band of 6 per cent around its central rate of DM2.95. Its range was therefore DM3.13 to DM2.77. Prime minister Thatcher was a reluctant convert to the ERM. Her personal economic advisor, Sir Alan Walters, had long argued that it was a fundamentally flawed system
- **Stage Two** By 1 January 1994 all currencies to have entered the narrow band (2.25 per cent) of the ERM. A European Monetary Institute to be established as the forerunner of a European Central Bank
- **Stage Three** Four convergence criteria are deemed necessary for countries wishing to participate in the third stage of EMU, when a single European currency will be established and an independent European Central Bank set up to run monetary policy. They are:
  - Price stability: average inflation rate to be within 1.5 per cent of three best performing member states
  - Non-excessive government deficits: deficits not to exceed 3 per cent of annual GDP; total accumulated government debt not to exceed 60 per cent of GDP
  - Stable currency: narrow band ERM participation for two years without devaluation
  - Low interest rates: average long-term nominal rate of interest to be within 2 per cent that of three best performing member states.

A deadline of 31 December 1996 is set for the European Council to agree a date for the third stage of EMU. If, by the end of 1997, no date has been agreed then the third stage of EMU must, according to the provisions of the Maastricht Treaty, begin on 1 January 1999. At Maastricht the British and Danes secured a possible opt-out from this third stage of EMU.

However, the Maastricht timetable was thrown into disarray by the severe pressure faced by the ERM in 1992 and 1993. The main reason for strain was German reunification, which generated inflationary pressures in Germany and consequent high interest rates. By rising on foreign exchanges the Deutschmark placed intense pressure other ERM currencies. Economies in recession or struggling to emerge from it – such as the British, Spanish and French – were forced to maintain high interest rates in order to sustain their ERM parities, even though such policies neglected the needs of their real economies.

Before too long, high interest rate policies began to lose credibility with financial markets. Speculators eagerly took the opportunity provided by the looming French referendum of 20 September 1992 to test the resolve of policy makers. On the morning of 16 September – 'black' or 'golden' Wednesday, according to taste – a vast amount of money moved out of sterling and into Deutschmarks. The British government refused to countenance devaluation and raised interest rates from ten to 15 per cent to try to attract dealers back to sterling. However, the speculative pressure could not be stemmed, and sterling 'floated' out of its ERM band. It was an effective devaluation, as rather than floating sterling sunk. In Italy the government was beset with budget problems and the lira, which had been 'revalued' only days earlier, followed sterling out of the ERM. Spain opted for devaluation within the ERM and, along with Ireland, imposed exchange controls in an attempt to curb speculative pressures.

The following week the franc came under sustained pressure and was saved only by heavy Bundesbank backing. For the time being, plans for EMU were kept on track. However, renewed pressure in July 1993 proved to be irresistible. On 1 August 1993 EC finance ministers gave up the struggle to sustain the ERM in the face of sustained speculative pressure against the franc in particular. Fluctuation bands were widened to 15 per cent for all participating currencies except the Deutschmark and Dutch guilder, which remained within narrow bands. The central purpose of the ERM – exchange rate convergence as part of broader plan for EMU – was thereby undermined. Although its infrastructure remains in place, the possibility of a return to narrow bands appears to be remote.

The ERM crisis damaged the Franco-German axis which has long sustained the EC. After the franc's humiliation, the French felt that Germany had neglected European interests by focusing on domestic priorities and refusing to cut its interest rates. The crisis also raised the possibility of competitive devaluations within Europe, and maybe a return protectionism. In sum, prospects for the single market and progress towards EMU were no longer good. Yet the case for a single currency remains strong. 'If sceptics and enthusiasts alike agree on the benefits of the single market, they must also acknowledge the case for stable currencies, however achieved.'[4]

The Maastricht criteria for EMU are now unattainable within the timetable envisaged. What may emerge in their place is a two-speed

EC. In August 1993 the Germans and Dutch have maintained their narrow band parities and could proceed rapidly to a single currency. Other states could perhaps join them at a later date. France, Belgium, Denmark and Luxembourg may all have this intention, though whether they will ever have sufficiently strong and stable currencies remains open to question.

SOCIAL POLICY

Having considered one contentious area of EC policy it is time to investigate an area that causes particular problems for the British Conservative government. It believes EC social policy imposes regulations on business that are likely to reduce competitiveness in world markets. By contrast, the other 11 member governments believe enforcement of minimum social standards to be a necessary corollary to freedoms given to business by the SEA. At Maastricht Britain secured an opt-out from the agreement on social policy signed by the other 11 member states.

EC social policy existed prior to Maastricht. Indeed, Britain has already agreed to a series of social policy provisions contained in the Treaty of Rome and supplemented by the SEA. These include measures relating to free movement of workers, right of establishment, approximation of laws, health and safety protection, dialogue between management and labour, equal pay for men and women, vocational training, and economic and social cohesion.

Development of social policy has been a continuous theme in the EC's evolution. In 1969 German Chancellor Willy Brandt submitted a memorandum on social policy to the Hague summit arguing that economic integration necessitated social action. In 1972 the Paris summit endorsed the idea of a Social Action Programme which, when launched in 1974, generated attempts to tackle gender inequality. More ambitious proposals have, however, been blocked. One such was the Vredeling directive on the rights of workers to information about their companies.

In 1985 new Commission President Jacques Delors decided to relaunch the 'social dialogue'. A meeting was held at Val Duchesse, a chateau in the south of Belgium. Pressure for social action came from member states which feared their high standards of social provision could make them uncompetitive in a single market (Table 5.1). Once capital can move freely industry may relocate to places where labour is cheap, a process known as 'social dumping'.

Table 5.1 Expenditure on social protection in EC member states, 1989

	% of GDP
Netherlands	30.2
Denmark	29.6
France	27.7
West Germany	27.6
Belgium	26.8
Luxembourg	25.6
Italy	23.1
UK	20.7
Ireland	20.3
Spain	17.3
Portugal	16.6
Greece	16.3

Source *Eurostat* (OOP, Luxembourg, 1991)

In fact, two principal justifications for Community social policy can be advanced:

● **Ideological** Christian Democratic and Social Democratic parties tend to adhere to ideas of 'social solidarity' which seek to build consensus between employers and employees. This conflation of economic and social progress is seen by them as the cornerstone of European economic success in the post-war era and as a necessary condition of future progress

● **Pragmatic** High social costs could lead both to uncompetitiveness and to increased unemployment. However, it is argued that the adoption of minimum standards across the Community could reduce this risk by preventing countries from gaining competitive advantage by lowering their standards of social protection.

The British government has never been convinced by either argument. It sees the single market as an end in itself, not as a means to an end (particularly when that end contrasts so markedly with policies being pursued at the national level). For it, EC social policy is the key which could lock the gate of 'fortress Europe'. An over-regulated and uncompetitive EC would then risk either higher levels of unemployment in an open world trading order, or imposition of protectionist measures to preserve EC employment levels.[5]

Indeed, on these grounds some British Conservatives apparently welcome the prospect of a two-tier Europe. They have visions of a deregulated and opted-out British economy out-performing the over-regulated, corporatist core. They point to Britain's high level of inward investment from Japan as proof of competitiveness. In 1990 Britain attracted Japanese investment worth Ecu 2388 million. The equivalent French figure was Ecu 853 million. The German was Ecu 417 million. Britain was, in fact, by far the largest recipient of Japanese investment in the Community. However, the key point is that Japanese companies' decisions to locate in Britain are linked to single market access.

THE SOCIAL CHARTER

British protests notwithstanding, EC plans for the social domain increased in 1989 when the Commission brought forward its Community Charter on the Fundamental Social Rights of Workers: the Social Charter. The Charter does not have legal effect. It is simply a 'solemn declaration' signed by 11 member states in Strasbourg in December 1989. Britain refused to sign. It outlines rights for workers under 12 headings:[6]

1 Freedom of movement: workers must be allowed to engage in any profession or occupation in the Community
2 Employment and remuneration: all employees must be fairly remunerated
3 Improvement of living and working conditions: each worker has, for example, a right to a weekly paid rest period and paid annual leave
4 Social protection: adequate social protection and social security benefits
5 Freedom of association and collective bargaining: employers and workers have the right of association
6 Vocational training: every worker should have access to vocational training and be able to benefit from further training during his/her working life
7 Equal treatment for men and women
8 Information, consultation and participation of workers: this applies particularly to companies established in more than one member state
9 Health protection and safety at work: satisfactory health and safety conditions in the working environment

10 Protection of children and young people: minimum age of employment not lower than 15, plus limits on the amount of work-time and prohibition of night work

11 Elderly persons: a decent standard of living after retirement

12 Disabled persons: measures to improve their social and professional integration.

In many ways the Charter crystallises divisions between the British Conservative government and other member states. However, it can be argued that other member states were also unenthusiastic, but chose to hide their real feelings behind untarnished Euro-credentials and rely on Britain to block social policy proposals. Margaret Thatcher saw in the Social Charter not the moderation of mainstream European Christian Democracy but remnants of Britain's old system of industrial relations with 'beer and sandwiches' for trade union leaders at 10 Downing Street. She was not prepared to invite union leaders in through the front door of Number 10 and was determined that they would not gain entry through a 'back door' opened by Brussels.

THE SOCIAL CHAPTER

Prime Minister Major followed his predecessor by opposing any extension of Community social policy. Given the nature of the party he led, there was little room for him to do anything else. Major secured an opt-out from the Social Chapter of the Maastricht Treaty, claiming 'game, set and match for Britain'. The Social Chapter, embodying rights outlined in the Social Charter, became simply an agreement between the other 11 EC member states.

Under Article 2 of the Social Chapter the Council of Ministers can issue directives, adopted by QMV, on improvement of the working environment, health and safety, working conditions, information and consultation of workers, equality between men and women, and occupational integration. In areas such as social security, redundancy protection and the representation and defence of collective worker and employer interests the Council must act by unanimity. Provisions on pay and the right to strike or impose lockouts are excluded from the Social Chapter.

Britain's opt-out from the Social Chapter could lead EC member states into a legal minefield. If an EC national from another member state takes advantage of single market provisions for free movement of labour and seeks employment in Britain, will his or her rights as a citizen of the European Union be infringed by Britain's decision not to adhere to all aspects of Community social policy? Will British ministers be allowed to participate in Council discussions on social policy?

There is also the possibility that Britain will in any case be forced to adopt further aspects of EC social policy. In June 1993 the Commission proposed legislation on a maximum 48-hour working week throughout the EC. It did so under Article 118A of the SEA by arguing that long hours could endanger health and safety. The result is that the proposal will be decided by QMV, which could generate a British defeat. The British government intends to challenge the Commission's action by arguing that social policy is being introduced illegitimately. The essence of its case is procedural, though it is clear that its main concern is substantive. In the eyes of the British government, legislation on a maximum working week would represent an unwarranted denial of individual freedom.

MAASTRICHT'S OTHER INNOVATIONS

Four other policy areas are drawn into the range of Community competence by Maastricht:
- **Education** Agreement was reached on the need for an enhanced Community role in vocational training. The Treaty aims to stimulate more mobility between instructors, training agencies and firms as well as student, youth and teacher exchanges. It also seeks mutual recognition of diplomas between member states
- **Culture** Article 128 states that: 'The Community shall contribute to the flowering of the cultures of the member states, while respecting their regional and national diversity and at the same time bringing the common cultural heritage to the fore'
- **Public health** The EC will extend its current role in this sphere by seeking to tackle drugs dependence, promote research in the fight against disease and ensure that legislation takes account of public health effects
- **Trans European Networks** These seek to allow all parts of the Community to benefit from the internal market through the development of transport, telecom and energy infrastructures.

MAASTRICHT'S INTERGOVERNMENTAL 'PILLARS'

The Maastricht Treaty combines supranationalism and intergovernmentalism. Responsibilities are shared between member states and supranational institutions. In the spheres of foreign affairs, defence policy, home affairs and justice policy the member states have decided to proceed through intergovernmental cooperation. Supranational institutions will therefore be peripheral to decision processes in these spheres.

The Community created by the Maastricht Treaty is likened to a Greek temple with three pillars. First, there is the Community 'pillar' within which policies are subject to the involvement of supranational institutions. The two flanking pillars operate by means of intergovernmental cooperation in the spheres of justice and home affairs on the one side, and foreign and security policy on the other.

Nearly 30 years ago Hoffmann contended that integration would falter when it had to deal with matters of 'high politics' such as foreign affairs and defence.[7] Member states have sought to resolve this problem through intergovernmental cooperation. This cooperation is subject to review in 1996 when both flanking pillars may be incorporated within the supranational Community system.

THE COMMON FOREIGN AND SECURITY POLICY PILLAR

In 1970 the member states of the EC instigated foreign policy cooperation, known as European Political Cooperation (EPC). EPC attempted to establish an external profile to match the EC's burgeoning economic power and ensure, where possible, coordination. In 1986 the SEA strengthened EPC by establishing a secretariat to support its operations. The Maastricht Treaty boldly declares in Article J that: 'a common foreign and security policy is hereby established'. In reality the common foreign and security policy (CFSP) pillar is a formalisation of existing EPC procedures.

When Maastricht is ratified foreign and security policy will be decided by a system of 'joint action', but unanimity will continue to be the *modus operandi*. However, once 'joint action' has been agreed in principle, majority voting can be used for measures of detail. Any decision (say) to commit troops must therefore be made unanimously. Subsequent decisions about numbers involved, and so on, can be decided by qualified majority.

These provisions represent a development of intergovernmental coop- eration as earlier formalised in the West European Union (WEU), the European constituent of NATO. In the 1980s the French and Germans were keen to establish a stronger European defence profile. They intensified their own cooperation by setting up the 4000-strong Franco-German brigade, based in Bavaria. Other nations remained wary.[8] The Maastricht CFSP 'pillar' will strengthen the WEU. It is to move its secretariat to Brussels, set up a planning unit and invite all non-WEU members of the European Community (Denmark, Greece and Ireland) to join. The European Council and Council of Ministers, acting unanimously, will be central decision-making authorities for both foreign and defence policy.

War in the former Yugoslavia has been a severe test for Community foreign policy. The apparently unending carnage and chaos in Bosnia indicates that the EC has failed the test. Over 500 000 people have been killed in the civil war and two million people have been made refugees. Throughout, the USA has urged Europeans to take the lead in mediating a peaceful solution to a European problem. Yet by 1993 the war's scope and intensity appeared to be beyond the ability of the Community to resolve. All that was left of its peace-making initiative was Lord Owen's role as an EC-appointed mediator. In June 1991, after brokering another short-lived ceasefire, Luxembourg's foreign minister, Jacques Poos, had proclaimed 'This is the hour of Europe'. By 1993 the Community's failure to resolve a bitter dispute on its doorstep had proved a chastening experience. The economic strength of the Community serves as a useful asset in peacetime but offers little in the face of bitter ethnic and religious dispute.

THE JUSTICE AND HOME AFFAIRS PILLAR

The third pillar of the European Union deals with interior policy. The Trevi Group of interior ministers has in fact been meeting since the mid 1970s. In the mid 1980s the SEA gave an impetus to further cooperation by removing internal border checks and thereby height- ening the need for cross-border cooperation to tackle issues like immi- gration, asylum policy, international crime and drug trafficking.

The Dutch government's original draft of the Maastricht Treaty argued that these policy areas should be incorporated within the supranational structures of the Community. The British government resolutely opposed this, arguing that member states should retain ultimate authority over such matters. The following areas are recognised by the justice and home affairs (JHA) agreement as matters of common concern (Article K1):

- Border controls, asylum and immigration policy
- Combatting drug trafficking
- International fraud and cooperation on civil and criminal matters
- Customs cooperation
- Police cooperation – a European Police Office (Europol) has been set up to provide a Community-wide information exchange system on international crime.

On immigration policy EC members are adopting a restrictionist stance with tough border controls. Simultaneously, there is only limited Community action, mainly instigated by the European Parliament, to tackle the problems of racism and neo-fascism that bedevil many member states.[9]

A little light is cast on this rather shadowy world of intergovernmental cooperation by member states' annual reports on their activities to the European Parliament. The sensitivity of both CFSP and JHA means that intergovernmental cooperation is preferred to supranationalism and the involvement of Community institutions. One consequence of this is that these policy areas slip into a grey area of democratic accountability between the national and supranational level and thereby reinforce the Community's 'democratic deficit'.

A SETBACK FOR INTEGRATION?

The Maastricht Treaty lumbered through a tortuous process of ratification in member states. It took two referenda and a plethora of opt-outs for the Danes to sign the Treaty. In France the referendum campaign reflected the mood of discontent with an unpopular government and Maastricht only scraped through by 51 per cent to 49 per cent. In Britain the word Maastricht became synonymous with tedious Parliamentary disputes as the ratification process dragged on for over a year. In the end, ratification was only secured by means of a vote of confidence in John Major's government. In Germany the

Maastricht Treaty faces a legal challenge and may not be ratified until the end of 1993. It was ironic that the British government formally ratified the Maastricht Treaty on 2 August 1993 at the precise moment when its central feature – movement towards EMU – was destroyed by effective collapse of the ERM. The centrepiece of the Treaty was thereby revealed as flawed. Maastricht may not as integrationist as was first thought. However, the Treaty does extend EC policy competence in a number of important areas, and may hasten the emergence of a two-speed EC with a core group of countries, led by Germany, moving rapidly to EMU.

Yet Maastricht was never meant to be a blueprint for a federal Europe. Rather it reflected the sectoral federal approach of integration by stealth with a 'spillover' effect creating an integrative 'logic'. The events of 1992 and 1993 showed that spillover from the single market to EMU was far from logical, and that EC political and economic élites seeking to build an integrated Community had constructed their edifice on shaky foundations.

NOTES

1 HMSO, *Treaty on European Union* (HMSO, London, 1992).
2 D Swann, *The Economics of the Common Market*, sixth edition (Penguin, Harmondsworth, 1988).
3 Committee for the Study of Economic and Monetary Union, *Report on Economic and Monetary Union in the European Community* (OOP, Luxembourg, 1989).
4 *Economist*, 7 August 1993.
5 S George, *Britain and European Integration Since 1945* (Blackwell, Oxford, 1991), p.60.
6 European Commission, *Fundamental Charter of the Basic Social Rights of Workers* (OOP, Luxembourg, 1990).
7 Hoffmann, op cit.
8 During the Danish referendum campaign in June 1992 fears of conscription into a European army are thought to have swung some voters into the 'No' camp.
9 G Ford, *Fascist Europe* (Pluto Press, London, 1992).

6 COMMUNITY POLICIES

There is no typical EC policy sector. Each is shaped according to particular circumstances, notably the amount of autonomy member
states have been willing to cede to the Community. Article 2 of the
Treaty of Rome outlines EC objectives, the central aspect of which is
attainment of the single market. Article 3 then describes activities the
Community shall undertake to achieve its objectives.[1] This chapter
analyses the Community's budget, or 'own resources'. It then examines EC agricultural and regional policies, and looks at some of the
ways in which EC membership has affected the lives of British people.
The impact is often extensive.

THE BUDGET

In 1993 the EC budget amounted to Ecu 69 billion (£53 billion). This
sounds like, and indeed is, a very large sum of money. However, as a
proportion of the total Gross National Product (GNP) of all member
states, the EC's budget amounts to just 1.2 per cent. Only around 3.5
per cent of total member state budgets is accounted for by the EC.

The EC's budgetary process was created by a 1970 Treaty which
established three sources for the Community's 'own resources'. In
1988 the revenue base of the Community was expanded to take in a
fourth 'own resource'. The Community is not a club to which members pay a subscription. It is a Community with financial independence. The sources of Community funding are as follows:
● Customs duty levies on imports to member states collected on
trade with non-Community countries
● Levies on agricultural trade with non-member countries. These differ from customs duties in that they are not levied at a fixed rate.
Instead they fluctuate, and are designed to raise the price of imported
agricultural goods relative to those prevailing in the EC
● A proportion of member states' Value Added Tax (VAT) raised from
1 per cent to 1.4 per cent in 1986
● An amount proportional to each member state's share in total
Community GNP.[2]

In 1992 the levy on VAT provided the bulk of the Community's funding, 55 per cent in total. The GNP levy was the next largest component of the budget at 22.7 per cent. Customs duties amounted to 18.6 per cent of the budget. Agricultural levies were the smallest source at 3.7 per cent.

These are the financial resources at the Community's disposal: what does it spend its money on? The answer is relatively simple: traditionally agriculture, and increasingly the regions. In 1988 an agreement between EC institutions allowed a financial perspective to be developed. It sought to control the proportion of the budget spent on supporting farmers, and to increase the amount of money devoted to less developed regions of the Community. Regional aid – or what are known as EC structural funds – increased from 12.5 per cent to 25 per cent of the Community budget between 1988 and 1992 in a bid to promote what is known in Community parlance as 'economic and social cohesion'.

The 1988 agreement outlined the rate of growth of the Community budget as a proportion of Community GDP over a five-year period from 1988 to 1992 as follows: 1988: 1.15; 1989: 1.17; 1990: 1.18; 1991: 1.19; 1992: 1.20. This agreement was extended at the Edinburgh summit in December 1992 when a financial perspective to take the Community through to the end of the century was agreed. Table 6.1 below shows how the EC plans to spend its money between 1993 and 1999.

Table 6.1 Community budget allocations, 1993-99[1]

	1993	1994	1995	1996	1997	1998	1999
Agriculture	35230	35095	35722	36364	37023	37697	38389
Regions	21277	21885	23480	24990	26526	28240	30000
Internal policies[2]	3940	4084	4323	4520	4710	4910	5100
External policies[3]	3950	4000	4280	4560	4830	5180	5600
Administration	3280	3380	3580	3690	3800	3850	3900
Reserve	1500	1500	1100	1000	1100	1100	1100
Total	**69177**	**69944**	**72485**	**75224**	**77989**	**80977**	**84089**

1 1992 prices
2 Expenditure on research and development will account for between one half and two thirds of this sum
3 The main external policies of the Community are concerned with development aid, agriculture and trade
Source European Commission, *Bulletin of the European Communities* (OOP, Luxembourg, 1993)

The Edinburgh agreement for the 1990s will raise the EC budget from 1.2 per cent of total EC GNP in 1992 to 1.27 per cent by 1999. Although this is an important increase it is less than the 1.37 per cent Commission President Delors had hoped for. Agricultural expenditure will continue to decline as a proportion of the budget: from 56 per cent in 1992 to 46 per cent in 1999. Meanwhile spending on the regions will rise: from 25 per cent in 1992 to 35 per cent in 1999.

Arguments over the budget beset, and threatened to derail, the Community in the 1980s. Britain sought a budget rebate that was finally agreed at the Fontainebleau summit in June 1984. In 1980 and 1985 the European Parliament rejected the Commission's proposed budget, and in 1984, 1985 and 1988 the budget had to be topped up by additional national contributions. The financial perspectives agreed in 1988 and 1992 have generated a more harmonious relationship between budgetary authorities, but there is still the possibility of future problems, particularly in a recessionary era.

The Commission proposes the budget to two joint budgetary authorities, the Parliament and the Council of Ministers. The Council has the final say on what is known as *compulsory expenditure*, which is that related to the original purposes of the Community as set out in the Rome Treaty. In the main, this is agricultural expenditure. The European Parliament has the final say on *non-compulsory expenditure*, which is that spent on areas into which the EC has moved since the founding Treaties. In the main, this is regional aid. As the proportion of the budget spent on agriculture declines, and that spent on regions increases, so the authority of the European Parliament expands.

AGRICULTURE

Initially, the CAP was seen as an EC success, as its phased introduction by 1968 marked the establishment of a supranational decision-making process in an important area of economic activity. However, the proportion of the EC budget spent on agriculture is currently declining. By the end of this century it will have fallen to 45 per cent from the 80 per cent registered at the end of the 1970s. The paramount reason for this reduction is wastefulness and inefficiency. Throughout the Community the CAP has become infamous for butter mountains, wine lakes and the like.

Article 39 of the Treaty of Rome outlined five objectives for the CAP: to increase agricultural productivity; to ensure a fair standard of living for the agricultural community; to stabilise markets; to assure the availability of supplies; and to ensure reasonable prices to consumers. These objectives were to be attained by institution of common prices for agricultural produce within the Community. Prices are decided annually by the Council of Ministers in the first half of the year, on the basis of proposals made by DG VI of the Commission. The weakness of the system is that prices have tended to be set too high, leading to over-production. The system stimulates over-production and a build-up of agricultural surpluses.

One reason for high price levels is the political power of farmers. Agricultural interest groups are highly influential at both domestic and supranational level. The Committee of Professional Agricultural Associations (COPA) has around 50 full-time staff in Brussels. These are supplemented by full-time officials of national associations, of which the British National Farmers' Union (NFU) has between five and ten. The activities of agricultural lobby groups are not countered by groups of commensurate strength representing consumer or environmental interests, and therefore tend to predominate

The CAP has developed a reputation for wastefulness, high prices and protection of farmers' interests. Typically large-scale farmers have profited from the system at the expense of consumers who must pay higher prices. Holland argues that the CAP has been a victim of its own success as it set out to try to increase productivity and promote self-sufficiency and has done so, admittedly at the cost of high prices and surpluses.[3] Perhaps this view is overly charitable: if the CAP represents success, then failure would be a sight to behold. In the 1980s the Commission embarked on a programme of reforms to try to curb the acknowledged excesses of the CAP.

The CAP can be assessed in terms of the five objectives laid out by Article 39 of the Treaty of Rome:
● **Increased productivity** Agricultural productivity has increased markedly, partly as a result of technological developments and partly as a consequence of the stimulation to production provided by the CAP. A consequence of this has been food surpluses. In 1991 20 million tonnes of cereals, one million tonnes of dairy products and 750 000 tonnes of beef contributed to a surplus stock valued at Ecu 3.7 billion. In addition, the policy has benefited large-scale

producers as the CAP's income support is largely proportionate to volume of production and, consequently, concentrates the greater part of support on larger, more intensive farms. In 1991 6 per cent of cereals farms accounted for 50 per cent of surface area and 60 per cent of production, whilst 15 per cent of dairy farms produced 50 per cent of milk and 10 per cent of beef farms had 50 per cent of beef cattle. Overall 80 per cent of support provided by the CAP's budget mechanism – the European Agricultural Guidance and Guarantee Fund (EAGGF) – was diverted to 20 per cent of farms

● **Ensuring a fair standard of living for the agricultural community** Per capita purchasing power of those engaged in agriculture improved very little in the 1970s and 1980s. This lack of improvement was compounded by the fact that over the same period the EC's active agricultural population fell by 35 per cent, whilst EAGGF expenditure increased from Ecu 4.5 billion in 1975 to Ecu 31.5 billion in 1991 (Ecu 11.5 billion at 1975 prices)

● **Stabilisation of markets** EC agricultural markets have been far more stable than world markets. However, if stability is associated with attainment of market equilibrium, then large surpluses would indicate instability

● **Provision of certain supplies** The CAP was created at a time when Europe was in deficit for most food products. Today, the EC is self-sufficient in most staple indigenous crops

● **Ensuring a fair price for the consumer** A principal failing of the CAP is that food prices in the EC have outstripped those on world markets. By the early 1980s the prices of wheat and barley were around 40 per cent above world levels, beef was 90 per cent above the world price level, and butter was 180 per cent more expensive in the EC than in the rest of the world.

The expense of the CAP generated pressure for reform. In the 1980s the British, Dutch and Danish governments were instrumental in pushing for improvement of the system as they had small and relatively efficient agricultural sectors which gained little from the policy (Table 6.2, overleaf). The impetus for reform was strengthened by the accession of Greece, Portugal and Spain in the 1980s, all of which have relatively large agricultural sectors which place additional strain on the CAP. Further enlargement of the Community in the 1990s could generate yet more pressure for reform, either from EFTA countries with efficient agricultural industries, or as a result of the absorption of inefficient sectors in central and eastern Europe.

Table 6.2 Agricultural efficiency of EC member states, 1991[1]

Country	% Employment	% GDP	Ratio
Netherlands	4.5	4.0	89
Belgium	2.7	2.1	78
UK	2.2	1.4	71
Luxembourg	3.1	2.2	71
Ireland	13.8	9.5	69
Denmark	5.5	3.7	67
Greece	21.6	13.9	64
France	5.8	3.3	57
FRG	3.3	1.5	45
Spain	10.7	4.6	43
Italy	8.5	3.6	42
Portugal	17.5	5.3	30
EC12	**6.2**	**2.9**	**47**

1 Agricultural 'efficiency' is calculated by dividing GDP devoted to agriculture by percentage employment in agriculture, and by multiplying by 100
Source Calculated from ibid

A series of reforms was introduced in the 1980s. In 1984 milk quotas were initiated in order to reduce over-production. In 1985 an effective price cut for agricultural produce was agreed when the price package provided for an increase of 1.8 per cent compared to an inflation rate of 5.8 per cent. In 1986 the price increase was 2.2 per cent whilst inflation was 2.5 per cent. In 1987 a price freeze was introduced for cereals and vegetables.

In the light of the 1988 budget agreement a further series of reforms was agreed:
- **Stabilisers** production over limits led to price cuts, thereby making it uneconomic to expand production
- **Set-aside** farmers were subsidised to take land out of production
- **Co-responsibility levies** ostensibly to assist product marketing, in reality the levy is a tax on production.

In 1993 the Commission reported that the impact of reform had been minimal as surplus stocks had continued to rise. 'The reforms of the years 1985-88 have not been implemented and are themselves incomplete. It is not surprising that under these conditions the CAP finds itself once again confronted with a serious crisis.'[4] The system of price guarantees had led to over-production. Consequently surpluses grew whilst the in-built incentive to intensive methods of production caused environmental damage. The Community found itself paying more and more money to large-scale producers whilst generating no solution to general problems of low farm incomes.

A further package of reforms was therefore introduced in 1993. It sought to move away from a price support policy to direct aid for producers in a bid to reduce over-production. Its principal measures are:

- A major reduction in cereal prices of 29 per cent over three years
- More effective measures to manage supply, such as set-aside arrangements for arable land
- Introduction of a system of permanent compensatory aid to neutralise the negative effects on income caused by the decision to reduce prices for cereals, oil seeds and beef
- Development of an agri-environmental action programme to encourage farmers to adopt less polluting and more environmentally sensitive methods of production
- Financial incentives for farmers who agree to whole or partial afforestation of their land
- An early retirement scheme for farmers aged 55 or above.

The success of these reforms is central to the budgetary framework agreed in 1992 because reduction of agricultural expenditure as a proportion of the budget will allow increased expenditure on other policy areas, particularly regional development.

REGIONAL POLICY

The Treaty of Rome contained no specific commitment to regional policy, apart from a generalised concern to secure 'balanced economic expansion'. Pressure from Italy and Ireland led to creation of the European Regional Development Fund (ERDF) in 1975, with a budget of £540 million. The budget was doubled in 1977. However, increases in inflation and the severe impact of economic recession meant that this increase did not represent a real advance.

There are marked regional disparities within the EC. The poorest regions are: Ireland, southern Italy, Spain (particularly the south) and Portugal. If average EC GDP is set at 100, then average GDP in Portugal and Greece is about 55, in Ireland 67 and in Spain 75. In recent years the proportion of people living in regions in which GDP per capita is 25 per cent below the EC average has risen from

24 million (10 per cent) to 62 million (20 per cent). Disparities are even more marked within countries. Within the UK, Northern Ireland has a GDP per capita of less than 75 per cent of the Community average, which means that it qualifies for high levels of regional aid. In July 1993 Merseyside and the Scottish Highlands were also included within the Community's poorest regions which qualify for what is known as Objective One status. Some regions have suffered from severe structural adjustment because of the recent decline of manufacturing industry. In Britain, the north of England and Scotland have been hit hard. Germany, after reunification in 1989, has sought EC aid to promote economic reconstruction in the former GDR.

Pressure for expanded regional aid grew in the 1980s when Greece, Portugal and Spain entered the Community. In some ways increases in regional aid were a 'side-payment' to poorer EC states in order to secure their agreement to the single market deal.[5] These poorer countries were concerned that their infrastructural and skills bases were not sufficiently developed to allow them to compete effectively in the single market. The SEA added a new Title V on 'Economic and Social Cohesion'. The Maastricht Treaty charged the heads of government with establishing a Cohesion Fund to supplement the development effort within the Community. The fund was established at the Edinburgh summit in December 1992. It will provide an Ecu 14.5 billion pot into which the four poorest member states – Greece, Ireland, Portugal and Spain – can dip to facilitate transport and environmental infrastructural developments until the year 2000.

Three main sources of regional aid are available through EC structural funds:
● **EAGGF** money can be provided to guide inefficient farmers towards more viable activities
● **European Regional Development Fund** (ERDF) money, which consumes around 10 per cent of the budget, is increasingly targeted on infrastructural development in poorer regions
● **European Social Fund** (ESF) money is designed to assist the retraining of both youth and long-term unemployed and to seek their integration into the labour force.

In recent years the EC has sought closer coordination between structural funds. A Commission report published in 1990 laid out five new sets of criteria by which funds were henceforth to be allocated. Each related to objective aspects of regional economies. Bracketed figures show the breakdown of total structural fund expenditure of more than Ecu 60 billion between 1989 and 1993, and demonstrate that Objective One regions consume by far the largest proportion of funds:

- **Objective One** (63%): Promotion of regions lagging behind, in particular those with a GDP per capita of less than 75 per cent of the Community average
- **Objective Two** (12%): Conversion of regions affected by serious industrial decline
- **Objective Three** (12%): Reduction of long-term unemployment
- **Objective Four** (6%): Integration of young people into the labour force
- **Objective Five** (5%): Promotion of rural development following reform of the CAP.

The Commission has also sought in recent years to introduce a subjective element into structural fund allocations. Instead of relying entirely on sets of 'objective' figures – levels of GDP, unemployment, and so on – it now encourages regions to make a case for receipt of assistance. The fact that this case must be made at the regional level evidently poses problems within England, which has no elected regional tier of government. It has prompted both private and public sector institutions to seek enhanced regional coordination. In the North West, for example, a North West Regional Association (NWRA) has been formed. It brings together leading businesses, as well as elected local authorities, and is an explicit response to changes in the way in which EC structural funds are allocated. The NWRA's most important venture to date is production of a regional economic strategy, to which all partners are committed.

By means of its developing regional policy the Commission is slowly building a network of regional partners. Organisations like the NWRA have direct links into DG XVI, which handles regional policy. Regional authorities in the rest of Europe, which tend to be much more developed, have still better contacts. The result is a series of links which permit the Commission and European regions to begin to by-pass possibly reluctant member states (such as the British). At present, member state agreement is necessary before anything can be made of these contacts: national governments are still important gatekeepers on the European scene. Nevertheless, it is increasingly possible to talk meaningfully of an emergent 'Europe of the regions', particularly where member states have an established regional tier.

THE COMMUNITY IN ACTION

There are a number of other areas in which the Community has an impact on the lives of member states' citizens. Only three areas can be reviewed here. They are pensions, privatisation, and environmental regulation.

In the sphere of pensions, a 1989 ECJ decision (Barber vs Guardian Royal Exchange) means that equal retirement ages for men and women now have to be phased in across the Community. Currently, women in Britain retire at 60 and men at 65. Douglas Barber, a claims manager for GRE in Sheffield, died in 1989. In 1980 he argued before an industrial tribunal for equal treatment between the sexes in the pensions sphere. The ECJ cited Article 119 of the Treaty of Rome – which provides for equal pay for men and women – in upholding his claim. The decision in the Barber case was a legal landmark because it acknowledged that occupational pension schemes count as pay. It obliged the British government to set in train legal changes which will equalise retirement ages at 60. The cost will be enormous: pension funds estimate it at up to £2 billion pounds per annum. In future years, as the pressure of an ageing society is increasingly felt, there are likely to substantial problems in finding this extra money.

The British privatisation drive was one of Thatcherism's flagship policies. This too is now being affected by EC law. A 1977 EC directive on acquired rights for workers was incorporated into British law as the Transfer of Undertakings (Protection of Employment) (TUPE) regulation in 1981. TUPE could have a major impact on the policy of contracting out public sector work to private sector companies. It lays down that when an operation is privatised employees transfer to the new undertaking their original rights and conditions of employment. Redundancies can be treated as unfair dismissals. In the most recent round of market testing involving £1.5 billion worth of work, around 50 per cent of contracts have been won by private-sector companies. TUPE applies to a majority of them. Furthermore, the directive could apply retrospectively. In July 1993, 18 sacked refuse collectors in Hastings won an historic legal victory when the Employment Appeals Tribunal in London upheld their claim that their dismissal after local refuse services had been privatised contravened TUPE. Councils and other public sector employers, such as health authorities, could now face thousands of claims from workers who have lost their jobs or had inferior pay and conditions imposed as a result of contracting-out.

A further aspect of EC responsibilities is protection of the quality of the environment and promotion of rational natural resource use. This is a logical area for Community activity as pollution knows no boundaries and common action is necessary if degradation of the natural environment is to be combatted. The years 1973 to 1992 witnessed five Community environmental action programmes. They dealt with matters such as water quality, atmospheric pollution, noise, toxic waste and wildlife protection. The SEA confirmed the right of the EC to legislate on environmental issues, although by unanimity. Sustainable development is the aim of the fifth Community environment programme approved by the Council in December 1992, an ambition initially set out at the Rio Earth Summit in June 1992.

Britain has fallen foul of EC environmental regulations on a number of occasions. In October 1992 it was taken to the Court of Justice for failing to clean beaches at Blackpool, Formby and Southport within a reasonable period in line with a 1976 directive on purity of bathing waters. On 14 July 1993 the Court ruled that the beaches at Blackpool and Southport did not measure up to EC environmental standards. The Commission withdrew the complaint against Formby. Indeed, in 1992 it was estimated that only 79 per cent of Britain's beaches complied with the 1976 directive, making Britain the second worst offender in the EC, ahead only of Germany with 76 per cent compliance. All other countries registered over 90 per cent compliance, although *Holiday Which?* reported in August 1993 that some countries which claimed compliance were being economical with the truth.

The British road-building programme has also come into conflict with Community authority. In July 1993, in the face of determined opposition from environmentalists, the government abandoned a planned new trunk road linking the A2 (London to Dover) with the A406 (London North Circular). The proposed road would have destroyed the ancient Oxleas Wood in south-east London. The Commission initiated proceedings against the British government on the grounds that a proper environmental impact assessment, required by Community law, had not been carried out. The government, though, is pressing ahead with construction of the M3 extension across Twyford Down in Hampshire. Here too the ire of the environmental lobby was aroused, and again it discovered an ally in the Commission. Environment Commissioner Carlo Ripa di Meana initiated proceedings against the British government in June 1992. The action was, however, dropped one month later.

A CHANGE OF EMPHASIS

The Community's main concern continues to be support for the agricultural sector. However, the amount of money spent on agriculture is declining both as a proportion of the budget and in real terms. Increasingly, EC money is spent on poor regions of the Community (some of which are agricultural). This movement towards greater economic and social cohesion represents a shift away from the original market-based purposes of the Community. The EC now takes a wider responsibility for living standards of citizens of the European Union which it is trying to construct. Its policy impact is widespread.

NOTES

1 However, incorporation of a policy area into Article 3 does not mean that a common policy has been established. Article 3E calls for a common transport policy, but the Community has not yet managed to organise one.
2 This fourth source of funds is linked to the relative wealth of members, meaning that the rich pay more and that a redistributive element enters the Community's funding arrangements.
3 M Holland, *European Community Integration* (Pinter, London, 1993).
4 European Commission, 'The Development and Future of the CAP', *Bulletin of the European Communities*, Supplement 5/91 (OOP, Luxembourg, 1991), p.11.
5 A Moravscik, 'Negotiating the Single European Act', in Keohane and Hoffmann, op cit, ch.2.

7 A WIDER AND DEEPER COMMUNITY?

Throughout its history the Community has 'widened' as new members have joined. In 1973 Britain, Denmark and Ireland entered, followed by Greece in 1981 and Spain and Portugal in 1986. The Community further expanded when the former GDR entered the EC in 1990 as part of a reunified Germany. The Community has also 'deepened' as integration has proceeded by means of measures such as the SEA and the Maastricht Treaty (the precise impact of which is yet to be determined). In the 1990s processes of widening and deepening are likely to continue.

A WIDER COMMUNITY

Article O of the Maastricht Treaty states that 'Any European State may apply to become a Member of the Union. It shall address its application to the Council, which shall act unanimously after consulting the Commission and receiving the assent of the European Parliament, which shall act by an absolute majority of its component members'. The term 'European' has not been officially defined, but is seen as combining geographical, historical and cultural elements which all contribute to the European identity but cannot be condensed into a simple formula.

Prospective member states need to meet a series of criteria:
● Acceptance of the *acquis communautaire* (the objectives of the Community) as outlined in Article 2 of the Maastricht Treaty, covering the internal market, EMU, economic and social cohesion, the common foreign and security policy, citizenship provisions and cooperation on justice policy and home affairs
● Compatible economic structures, meaning a market-based economy. However, on entry the economic structures of Greece, Portugal and Spain were not very compatible with those of the rest of the Community. The Commission argued that the EC was 'making a commitment which is primarily a political one ... reflecting the concern of these three new democracies for their own consolidation and protection against the return of dictatorship and constituting an act of faith in a united Europe'. This could act as a precedent in years to come.

● Compatible political structures, meaning liberal democratic political systems and respect for the rule of law

● There is perhaps a concealed criterion: new accessions should not have adverse budgetary implications.[1] Recession in the 1990s may prevent rapid accession of poorer European countries which would place pressure on the Community budget.

EFTA, THE EEA AND COMMUNITY MEMBERSHIP

The countries which are at the front of the queue for EC membership are four of the seven EFTA member states. Norway, Sweden, Austria and Finland have applied for membership. Iceland, Liechtenstein and Switzerland have not. The EC and EFTA have developed an expansive web of economic links, and a high degree of interdependence has resulted. Together these two groupings account for over 30 per cent of world GDP and constitute by far the largest trading bloc, with close to 45 per cent of world trade. The EC and EFTA are each others' most important trading partners. The EFTA region is the destination for over 25 per cent of Community exports with a share greater than the US and Japanese markets combined.

In April 1984 the Luxembourg Declaration by EC and EFTA ministers expressed a desire for extended cooperation, in particular through free trade agreements. This declaration was consolidated in Oporto 1991 when the European Economic Area (EEA) was agreed, although the agreement was not signed until May 1992 after resolution of a dispute with the ECJ over legal jurisdiction. The EEA came into effect in 1993. It extends the four 'freedoms' – movement of people, goods, services and capital – of the EC's internal market to the seven members of EFTA and thereby creates a single market of 380 million people. The EEA document is fatter than the Treaty of Rome, weighing in at 100kg. It contains 15 000 pieces of Community legislation which EFTA countries must incorporate into their legal systems. Although the EEA is designed to maximise trading benefits, some EFTA countries are displeased that they must abide by EEA laws but are only allowed a consultative role in shaping them. (Similar concerns motivate the British desire to get to the 'heart' of Europe.) Consequently, the EEA has developed into a half way house to Community membership for Austria, Sweden, Norway and Finland.

Austria's membership application was lodged in July 1989. Austria would be one of the most stable and prosperous countries in the EC. In 1990 its GDP per capita was 13 per cent above the Community average. In terms of trade, Austria has been integrated into the Community for some time: the EC supplies 68 per cent of Austria's imports and takes 65 per cent of its exports. Not surprisingly, Germany is Austria's largest trading partner. The main stumbling bloc to accession is Austria's neutrality. Article 1 of the Austrian State Treaty of 1955 commits the country to 'perpetual neutrality', and prevents it from joining military alliances or allowing installation of foreign bases on Austrian soil. The end of the Cold War has permitted Austria to indicate a willingness to accept the *acquis* on foreign and security policy, although opinion polls indicate that many Austrians link their prosperity to the 1955 declaration.[2]

Sweden, with a population of 8.5 million, applied for membership in July 1991. It already implements a large part of the Community's *acquis* in spheres such as social and environmental policy, company law, consumer protection and competition rules. Sweden too is prosperous: its GDP per capita was 20 per cent higher than the Community average in 1990 (it had been 30 per cent higher in 1970). As is the case with Austria, the main problem with Swedish membership of the EC is a tradition of neutrality dating back to the nineteenth century. After the end of the Cold War the Swedish government declared that 'policy of neutrality' was no longer an adequate description. It prefers now to speak of 'Swedish foreign and security policy with a European identity'.[3]

In 1992, a Finnish government report concluded that its policy of neutrality was compatible with Community membership and an application was lodged. Norway, which is a member of NATO, has for many years had an ambivalent stance towards EC membership. With Britain, it had application bids rejected in 1963 and 1967. Again with Britain, a reapplication in 1970 was accepted and a treaty of accession signed in 1972. However, in a referendum in September 1972 the Norwegian people rejected membership: 53 per cent voted 'No'. Subsequently Norway's trade links with the Community have continued to intensify: by 1990 nearly 60 per cent of its trade was with the EC. In 1972 the Norwegians rejected membership because they feared isolation from their Scandinavian neighbours. In the 1990s not to join would be to risk isolation.

Fear of isolation has also concerned the Swiss government. However, the prospect of membership of a supranational organisation does not appeal to the Swiss people, who narrowly voted to reject membership of the EEA in a December 1992 referendum: 51 per cent were against, 49 per cent in favour. The remarkable aspect of this episode was not that the Swiss voted 'No', but that a country that does not even have a domestic single market should have applied for EC membership in the first place. In December 1992 a referendum in Liechtenstein approved membership of the EEA. Iceland has also joined the EEA but has ruled out an application for EC membership in the near future.

EXPANSION IN CENTRAL AND EASTERN EUROPE

The shifting sands of the European state system make it difficult to predict the political cartography of central and eastern Europe in the wake of the *annus mirabilis* of 1989 when the Soviet bloc crumbled. Accession to the EC of former Soviet bloc countries would present many more problems for the Community than would membership for EFTA countries. This is entirely because the economic profiles of the two groups are vastly different.

The G7 summit in Paris in October 1989 asked the Commission to coordinate a planned programme of economic aid for Poland and Hungary (PHARE). Other OECD member states supported this initiative and came together to form the G24 (12 EC countries, six EFTA countries, the USA, Canada, Japan, New Zealand, Australia and Turkey). In July 1990 the G24 agreed to extend the programme to the former GDR, Czechoslovakia (now split into two separate republics), Bulgaria and Yugoslavia. The PHARE programme has five priorities: access to donor countries' markets for goods produced by beneficiaries; development of agricultural and food industries; investment promotion; training; environmental protection.

The 1990 action programme, for which Ecu 500 million was set aside, included economic aid for Poland, Hungary, Czechoslovakia, Bulgaria and Yugoslavia, humanitarian aid for Romania, and two special programmes (one environmental and one regional for the former GDR). In 1991 money was made available to Poland (Ecu 192-212m), Hungary (Ecu 100-137m), Czechoslovakia (Ecu 88-105m), Bulgaria (Ecu 143-160m) and Romania (Ecu 80-110m). The 1992 budget for eastern Europe totalled nearly Ecu 1 billion.

In addition, *Europe Agreements* were concluded with Poland, Hungary and Czechoslovakia in December 1991, and subsequently with Bulgaria and Romania. By the end of the ten-year term of the agreements signatories are intended to be where EFTA countries were in 1993 in terms of trading arrangements with the Community. The preamble to the agreements makes the eventual intent quite clear: 'Having in mind that the final objective of [Poland/Hungary/Czechoslovakia] is to become a member of the Community and that this association ... will help to establish this objective'.

The main areas covered by *Europe Agreements* are political dialogue, free trade and freedom of movement, economic cooperation, financial cooperation, and cultural cooperation. Trade agreements have also been signed with the Baltic states (Estonia, Latvia and Lithuania), and with Albania.

SOUTHERN ENLARGEMENT

The third group of countries to seek EC membership are those on its southern flank: Turkey, Cyprus and Malta. In July 1987 Morocco applied for membership but was not considered to be a European country and the application was rejected.

Turkey first applied for EC membership in 1959 but its economic and political structures were not seen as compatible with membership. In 1963 a three-stage association agreement was signed in Ankara with a target date for accession of 1995. Turkey's last application for membership, in April 1987, came at a bad time as the Community was adjusting to three new members, a budget deficit and the move to a single market. The application was put on hold in 1989.

There are a number of problems with the Turkish accession bid, not the least of which is that Greece would veto Turkish entry while Cyprus remains divided. Turkey is also a very poor country. In 1989 GDP per capita stood at a mere 10 per cent of the Community average. In addition, over 40 per cent of the Turkish workforce is in the agrarian sector. The implications for EC regional and agricultural budgets of Turkish accession would seem to be immense. There could also be problems with the free movement provisions of the single market. Berlin already has the largest urban Turkish population after Ankara. Although Turkish workers were an essential element in West

Germany's economic success, they have been victims of a neo-Nazi backlash in the wake of reunification and economic recession.

Malta and Cyprus applied for Community membership in July 1987. The accession of Cyprus looks unlikely whilst the island remains divided between Greek and Turkish Cypriots. Despite endless rounds of negotiations since the Turkish invasion in 1974, resolution of the dispute still appears a distant prospect.

Both Cyprus and Malta have association agreements with the Community. A problem with the accession of both countries would be the impact of micro-states with 'city hall' governments. Would, for example, such small countries have the diplomatic resources necessary to assume the Council Presidency?

DEEPENING OF THE COMMUNITY

New accessions could place additional strain on both the institutional and policy structures of the Community, although EFTA states would be compatible with other Community members in terms of economic harmonisation. Further widening of the Community may lead to pressure for deepening of integration to ensure that the Community is not weakened by enlargement. The Commission has noted the need for deepening to accompany widening: 'Non-members apply to join because the Community is attractive; the Community is attractive because it is seen to be effective; to proceed to enlargement in a way that reduces its effectiveness would be an error'.[4]

There are two types of 'deepening': institutional deepening whereby the supranational structures of the Community are strengthened, and policy deepening of Community responsibilities. Even during the period of 'Eurosclerosis' in the 1970s deepening occurred. In 1970 European Political Cooperation was initiated. In 1975 the European Council met for the first time. In 1978 the EMS was set up. In 1979 direct elections to the European Parliament were held. In the 1980s the accession of Greece, Portugal and Spain was one of the factors that prompted reform of EC institutional structures, Use of majority voting was increased and policy integration was extended. A commitment to economic and social cohesion was made. Widening and deepening thus went hand in hand in the 1980s as consolidation of the Community's economic profile made membership an attractive proposition and the entry of new members prompted reform of institutional and policy structures.

Article N(2) of the Maastricht Treaty contains a provision for review of the Community's objectives in 1996 when further deepening may occur. In particular, there may be pressure for incorporation of the CFSP and JHA intergovernmental pillars in the Community's supranational remit. Widening would of course alter the balance of national interests within the Community. Scandinavian countries and Austria have high social and environmental standards which could prompt further pressure for deepening in these areas. Widening to the east and the south would bring poorer countries into the Community with attendant pressure on agricultural and regional funds.

Widening would also induce a re-evaluation of the Community's institutional structure. The range of issues covered by QMV could be increased to ensure that decision-making effectiveness in a wider Community was maintained. The number of MEPs would also need to be increased to take account of new members, although a European Parliament with nearly 1000 members may be so unwieldy as to make its chances of effectiveness minimal. Pressure to streamline the Community's institutional structure could mean that not all new member states are allowed to appoint Commissioners.

NEW MEMBERS AND INSTITUTIONAL REFORM

A Community of 15 or 16 members by the mid 1990s is not unrealistic. Norway, Sweden, Austria and Finland seem poised for membership, depending on satisfactory completion and ratification (possibly by means of referenda) of accession negotiations. Politically and economically, each is compatible with the *acquis communautaire*, and seeks to share the economic success of the Community and prevent exclusion from the single market.

By 2003 a number of central and east European states would, if the *Europe Agreements* are a success, be on the verge of membership. Then the Community could expand to 20 members. At the same time, the Baltic states and western republics of the former Soviet Union may also be attracted to the economic colossus on their doorsteps. Creation of the single market has made the EC the central feature of the European political and economic landscape and has thereby drawn neighbouring states into its web of interdependence. Widening of the Community will prompt pressure for further institutional and policy deepening, for a political intent underpins the process of European integration. The dilemma for current members, particularly the six founders, is how to maintain integrative impetus in a wider Community.

NOTES

1 N Nugent, 'The Deepening and Widening of the European Community: Recent Evolution, Maastricht and Beyond', *Journal of Common Market Studies* 30 (1992), 311-28.
2 European Commission, 'Europe and the Challenge of Enlargement. Commission Opinion on Austria's Application for Membership', *Bulletin of the European Communities*, Supp 4/92 (OOP, Luxembourg, 1992).
3 European Commission, 'Europe and the Challenge of Enlargement. Commission Opinion on Sweden's Application for Membership', *Bulletin of the European Communities*, Supp 5/92 (OOP, Luxembourg, 1992).
4 European Commission, 'Europe and the Challenge of Enlargement', *Bulletin of the European Communities*, Supp 3/92 (OOP, Luxembourg, 1992), p.14.

8 BRITISH MEMBERSHIP ASSESSED

Chapter 3 investigated the EC policy of successive British governments. This chapter focuses on factors that have been instrumental in
shaping the attitudes of those governments. It also analyses the
'Europeanisation' of British economic and political life occasioned by
EC membership. The formal dimension of this change is incorporation
of EC law into British law. Informally, the process of integration mani-
fests itself in an array of economic, political, cultural and social link-
ages. There is strong evidence that the British economy is closely
connected with those of our European partners. Politically and socially
evidence of integration is less great.

ECONOMIC IMPACT OF MEMBERSHIP

The main feature of the Community Britain joined in 1973 was the
customs union established by the Treaty of Rome and the linked
aspiration to create a single market. Hope became reality on 1 January
1993 when the SEA's provisions were formally enacted. Intensified
links with the Community have drastically altered British trade patterns, which are now predominantly focused on the continent of
Europe (Table 8.1).

**Table 8.1 Structure of UK exports and imports by country and
region, 1958 and 1990**

	Exports		Imports	
	1958	1990	1958	1990
EC	21.7	52.6	21.8	51.0
Other European OECD	9.1	9.0	8.7	12.3
USA	8.8	12.6	9.4	12.7
Canada	5.8	1.8	8.2	1.7
Japan	0.6	2.6	0.9	5.4
Australia	7.2	1.6	5.4	0.7
Other	46.8	19.8	45.6	16.2

Source *European Economy* (OOP, Luxembourg, 1992)

In 1958 only 21.7 per cent of UK exports went to, and 21.8 per cent
of imports came from, the six EC member states, whilst trading links
with the Commonwealth countries of Australia and Canada were still

strong. By 1990 more than 50 per cent of Britain's exports and imports were either going to, or coming from, other EC member states, and Germany had overtaken the USA as Britain's leading trade partner. Links with Canada and Australia have declined substantially. In contrast with other member states, though, Britain has maintained strong trading ties with the USA and has increased trading links with Japan, thereby indicating a continued preference for global rather than strictly regional trading connections.

British accession meant acceptance of the CAP. By the late 1980s British consumers were paying around 20 per cent above world prices for their food. Britain, with its relatively small and efficient agricultural sector, has benefited little from the CAP and the British government has been to the fore in pressing for reform of the policy.

One area of marked comparative advantage for the British economy is its strong service sector. However, moves towards EC service industry liberalisation – in financial services and airlines, for example – have been slow. One of the major advantages for the British economy of the single market has therefore not yet been properly attained.

CONSTITUTIONAL IMPLICATIONS

The fundamental principle of Britain's unwritten constitution is parliamentary sovereignty. It has two main elements. First, statute law passed by Parliament overrides other sources of law. Secondly, the principle of *lex posterior derogat priori* (later law overrides earlier) means that no Parliament can bind its successor.

In its 1971 White Paper on the effects of membership the Heath government contended that 'There is no question of any erosion of essential national sovereignty'. A Labour MP begged to differ in the January 1972 debate on accession, and carried into the House of Commons 42 volumes containing 2500 EC regulations which would automatically become British law once Britain acceded to the Treaty of Rome.

In 1964 the ECJ had established the principle that EC law overrides national law (in the case of Costa vs ENEL). Thus, by joining the EC Britain became subject to two apparently contradictory principles: statute law passed by the supposedly sovereign British Parliament can be overridden by Community law. The judiciary resolved this problem by treating EC laws as rules of construction. Cases of conflict between EC and national law would then be assumed to be a consequence of parliamentary error as the legislature was not likely to seek to contravene supranational obligations which it had itself assumed.

SCRUTINY AND ACCOUNTABILITY

The British Parliament has had difficulty scrutinising EC legislation and holding governments to account for their activities at Community level. The 'democratic deficit' which exists supranationally is thereby compounded by weak democratic control at the national level.

A series of mechanisms has been created to secure accountability. The prime minister reports on meetings of the European Council to the House of Commons, and the report is then debated. Questions on EC policy can be addressed to the prime minister or departmental ministers during parliamentary questions. Select Committees can investigate Community matters that fall within their remit. The House of Lords has a committee on the EC which publishes detailed reports on Community activities. These have acquired a reputation for authoritativeness. In the House of Commons the Scrutiny Committee distinguishes more and less significant pieces of Community legislation, and recommends the more significant to the Commons for debate. However, these debates are often held late at night and are thus poorly attended. In 1989 the government supplemented the activities of the Scrutiny Committee by setting up three Standing Committees on EC affairs.

Despite this array of mechanisms, accountability is held to be lax. The House of Commons in particular needs to improve its scrutiny powers. It is currently deficient both in contributing to the development of EC policy, and in reviewing the progress of agreed policy.

THE IMPACT ON CENTRAL GOVERNMENT

The EC has increasingly impinged on the actions of central government as the operation of the British state is heavily influenced by Community membership in a number of policy sectors. The initial point of contact between the EC and the British government is frequently the UK's permanent representation in Brussels (UKREP).

UKREP services the work of the Council of Ministers through COREPER and can be very influential in the decision-making process. In 1989 Britain had one of the largest permanent representations in Brussels with 41 officials, compared to 44 West Germans, 34 French and 32 Italians. UKREP is supplemented by civil servants from British government departments who travel to Brussels when matters directly affecting their department are discussed.

Some departments of state, such as the Foreign and Commonwealth Office and Trade, have been in touch with the Community since its inception in 1951. For others, particularly the Ministry of Agriculture, Fisheries and Food (MAFF), membership of the Community has meant a fundamental reorientation of their activities as what were once national policies are now common policies determined at the supranational level. In 1982 the Permanent Secretary estimated that 200 MAFF officials went to Brussels every month. Community membership is becoming an issue of increased salience for a range of government departments, such as the Home Office, Education and Environment, as the EC's legal competence grows.

THE IMPACT ON LOCAL GOVERNMENT

A move towards a federal Europe would seem to imply an increased role for EC regions as, in accordance with the principle of subsidiarity, one would expect some powers to move to the supranational level and others to lower tiers of government. The role of regions within the EC will be enhanced by the new advisory Committee of the Regions established by the Maastricht Treaty.

This poses a particular dilemma for the British Conservative government. It is both an enthusiastic advocate of subsidiarity and presides over a system of local government the formal constitutional position of which is reflected in the principle of *ultra vires*. By this principle Parliament allocates functions to local government, and can just as readily take them away. The problem is compounded by the lack of an English regional tier to hand strategic functions to, and by Scottish and Welsh demands for independence. In 1992 both sub-nations set up a Brussels office: Scotland Europa and the Wales European Centre.

Some Directorate-Generals of the Commission, such as DG V (employment, industrial affairs and social affairs), DG XVI (regional policy) and DG XXII (coordination of structural policies), have been keen to promote links with EC regions. In addition, some British local authorities, such as Kent, Essex and Strathclyde, have developed European liaison departments and Brussels offices to ensure that they maximise the benefits of Community membership. Local authorities are also responsible for EC policy implementation for services such as consumer protection and waste disposal.

THE CONSERVATIVES AND EUROPE

Neither of the two main British parties has been consistently pro-European, and each is deeply divided on the issue. There are six main strands of Conservative thinking on Europe, though they should not be seen as mutually exclusive:

● **Tory traditionalists** adopt a 'neo-Gaullist' stance. They would like to see the Community operate along intergovernmental lines – a *Europe des patries* (Europe of nation states) as de Gaulle put it (although Tory traditionalists tend not to share de Gaulle's anti-Americanism). Thatcher enunciated this neo-Gaullist stance in her Bruges speech: 'My first guiding principle is this: willing and active co-operation between independent and sovereign states is the best way to build a European Community'[1]

● **Neo-liberals** favour a free market EC and are willing to cede some sovereignty in order to secure success for the single market. In doing so neo-liberals favour *negative* integration – bringing down barriers – rather than *positive* integration – creation of new formal structures.[2] In John Major's EC policy, and in Thatcher's acceptance of the SEA, there is a strong element of this neo-liberalism

● **Modernisers** believe EC membership can help Britain cast off the burdens of the past and recast itself as a modern and dynamic European power. Michael Heseltine and Edward Heath are proponents of this view

● **Federalists**, such as Harrow MP Hugh Dykes, would like to see a wholehearted endorsement of the integrative process. They are small in number and are linked to the federalist European Movement

● **Anti-marketeers**, again small in number, espouse an endemic hostility to European integration which they see as a threat to national identity. Enoch Powell, with his clear opposition to both European integration and immigration, is the intellectual progenitor of latterday anti-marketeers such as Nicholas Budgen

● **Pragmatists** are the biggest Conservative group. They adhere to a 'common sense Europeanism' and accept membership on pragmatic grounds. They can therefore be characterised as neither enthusiasts nor sceptics. Their utilitarian criteria may prevent development of wider public acceptance of the EC if political leaders fail to give clear guidance. Major has tried to portray himself as an arch-pragmatist over European integration in an attempt to appease party divisions.

Thatcher's September 1988 speech to the College of Europe in Bruges prompted creation of the Bruges Group as a clearing house for Tory Eurosceptics. Eurosceptics may belong to one of several strands identified above. They could be traditionalists, free marketeers or anti-marketeers. Their common point of reference is scepticism about moves towards a federal Europe. As Nicholas Ridley put it, the British people 'are determined to maintain their independence. In my view the British people would reject any government that sought to cede control of the country to a federal Europe'.[3]

LABOUR AND EUROPE

Between 1983 and 1992 the Labour Party transformed its stance on the EC. Its 1983 election manifesto, *New Hope for Britain*, contended that 'withdrawal from the Community is the right policy for Britain'. By 1992 its policy was one of enthusiastic endorsement. There are many strands of Euro-thought in the Labour Party:
● **Kinnockites/modernisers** are enthusiastic advocates of European integration. As party leader between 1983 and 1992 Neil Kinnock turned Labour away from hostility towards the EC in an attempt to restore its electoral appeal. The 1989 policy review document, *Meet the Challenge, Make the Change*, placed ERM membership at the heart of Labour's economic strategy. Current party leader, John Smith, is a firm member of this group, and was one of 69 Labour MPs to defy a three-line whip and vote in favour of accession to the Community in October 1971
● **Bennites** see the EC as a capitalist club which offers little to working people and would frustrate the actions of a Labour government. Tony Benn was a leader of the 'No' campaign in the 1975 referendum on British membership of the EC, and has remained hostile to the Community ever since. He was, however, marginalised during Kinnock's leadership, and has continued to be so by Smith

● **Nationalists,** such as Peter Shore and Michael Foot, are fearful of the implications of EC membership for national sovereignty, viewing it as an infringement of parliamentary sovereignty and thus a potential constraint on the actions of a future Labour government

● **The 'new left'** believes that the failure of the French Socialist government's attempted economic reflation in the early 1980s demonstrates that nation states can no longer act alone in the face of the transnational capitalism. It sees a reformed EC as the best route to socialism. Former GLC leader Ken Livingstone is a prominent member of this group

● **Pragmatists** are a large group in the Labour Party. They espouse a 'common sense Europeanism' which accepts Britain's EC membership but without real enthusiasm. Labour has come to be seen as the more 'European' of the two main parties. However, it seems likely that it is just as divided as are the Conservatives, but that its divisions have been obscured by opposition status.

ATTITUDES OF OTHER PARTIES

Within Britain the Liberal Democrats have been the most consistently European party. In their previous incarnation as the Liberal Party they urged membership of the ECSC in 1951 and of the EEC and Euratom in 1957. Furthermore, it was the anti-EC stance of the left-dominated Labour Party that prompted creation of the SDP and an eventual realignment of centre-party politics in Britain. In their 1992 general election manifesto the Liberal Democrats maintained their consistent line on European integration, calling for a federal Britain within a federal Europe.

The Scottish National Party (SNP) opposed membership of the EC until 1983. During the 1980s its attitude softened to the point at which, in 1988, it endorsed the EC under the slogan 'Scotland within Europe'. The SNP recognised that fear of isolation was a factor contributing to lack of support for independence and that anchoring Scotland to a federal Europe could allay it. It also realised the importance of Brussels as a source of aid for the Scottish economy, which has been hit hard by the decline in manufacturing industry. The SNP is now keen to develop links with other regionalist parties in Europe.

In Wales Plaid Cymru has been increasingly influenced by Green political thinking. It rejects the EC's defence role and the CAP whilst also advocating abandonment of free movement for capital and labour. The Green Party, which in 1989 took 14.9 per cent of the vote in European Parliament elections, but no seats, is very critical of the EC which it sees as developing into another nuclear superpower which puts economic growth before protection of the environment.

In Northern Ireland both main Unionist parties – the 'Official' Unionists (OUP) and the Democratic Unionists (DUP) – oppose membership of the Community, although each takes seats in the European Parliament to lobby on behalf of their part of Ulster's population. DUP leader, the Reverend Ian Paisley, has used his Strasbourg seat to denounce the Papist conspiracy that he sees as central to the Community. The nationalist Social Democratic and Labour Party (SDLP) endorses membership and has advocated an EC role in solving the Northern Ireland problem. The political wing of the Provisional IRA, Sinn Fein, is opposed to membership of the capitalist EC.

PRESSURE GROUPS AND THE EC

Pressure groups go where power goes: as power in a number of key sectors has gone to Community level, so pressure groups have re-focused their activities on the EC. This refocusing is an important part of the neo-functionalist integrative dynamic discussed in Chapter 1.

The first step for a national pressure group seeking to lobby at the supranational level is to find an analogous 'Eurogroup', of which there are over 500. Due to its small size and consequent lack of resources (time, money, expertise, and so on), the Commission is extremely attentive to the views of pressure groups. Within the EC policy process industrial and agricultural groups have tended to dominate.[4]

Within Britain the Confederation of British Industry (CBI) has been consistently pro-EC since the 1960s. It has its own Brussels office in the building which houses its EC analogue UNICE (a French acronym for the Union of Industries of the EC). In recent years the CBI has helped harden UNICE attitudes on Community social policies. At the domestic level the CBI worked closely with the Department of Trade and Industry to promote awareness of '1992', although it fell out with Thatcher's Conservative government over its firm endorsement of ERM membership.

The Trades Union Congress (TUC) now views the EC's responsibility for economic and social cohesion as a beacon of hope for a beleaguered labour movement. However, the trade unions spent most of the 1970s and 1980s in opposition to British membership. The turning point was Labour's electoral defeat in 1983 which prompted new 'realist' leaders, such as Bill Jordan of the Amalgamated Union of Engineering Workers (AUEW), to argue that trade unionists needed to make the Community work for them in the same way that industry had. The TUC's reorientation was confirmed by the wave of Euroenthusiasm which swept their 1988 conference when Commission President Jacques Delors received a standing ovation for his speech on the benefits of EC membership for the labour movement.[5]

PUBLIC OPINION

Although the main political parties have often failed to give a clear lead on European integration, other political institutions, such as local authorities and pressure groups, are increasingly looking towards the Community and playing a role in Britain's integration within Europe. British public attitudes to the EC are slowly changing as a result.

Opinion poll evidence suggests that the EC is a low salience issue in the minds of most British people, lagging far behind day-to-day concerns like inflation, unemployment and welfare. However, over time there has been a steady growth in the number of British people who are either very much, or to some extent, in favour of European unification. The level of 71 per cent in 1990 compares with 63 per cent in 1980. Only a small number of people are to some extent, or very much, opposed to the unification of Europe: 17 per cent in 1990, as opposed to 22 per cent in 1980. Britons are however less enthusiastic about Community membership than are other EC citizens (Table 8.2).

Table 8.2 Attitudes towards unification of western Europe in Britain and the EC, 1980-90

	1980		1985		1990	
	UK	EC9	UK	EC12	UK	EC12
For very much	23	27	30	35	27	35
For to some extent	40	46	38	42	44	45
Against to some extent	14	9	11	7	11	8
Against very much	8	4	4	3	6	3
No reply	15	14	17	13	12	9

Source *Eurobarometer Trends 1974-1990* (OOP, Luxembourg, 1991)

This difference is repeated when personal assessments of the costs and benefits of EC membership are collected (Table 8.3). In the UK the 1980s witnessed a trend increase in the number of people who think that membership has been beneficial, though again pro-EC sentiment lags behind that in the rest of the Community. The large increase in favourable responses between 1985 and 1990 coincides with resolution of Britain's budget dispute and launch of the single market programme, which received strong government support and good publicity.

Table 8.3 Personal assessments of costs and benefits of EC membership, 1980-90[1]

	1980		1985		1990	
	UK	**EC9**	**UK**	**EC12**	**UK**	**EC12**
Good thing	21	55	32	57	52	65
Bad thing	55	15	40	12	19	9
Neither	15	22	21	24	24	20
No reply	9	8	7	7	5	6

1 Individuals were asked whether they thought EC membership had been a good or bad thing
Source Ibid

Three main conclusions can be drawn from tables like these. First, there was a steady increase in UK support for European integration during the 1980s. Favourable publicity may account for much of this increase. Secondly, people in the UK tend to be less enthusiastic about European integration than people in other member states. Thirdly, there is a difference between *affective* and *utilitarian* support for the Community.[6] In Britain affective loyalty to the aspiration of European unity exceeds that of utilitarian support for the current form of unification (the EC).

A RELUCTANT EUROPEAN?

Increasing economic interdependence ties Britain to the EC and links British economic prospects to the collective endeavour of all member states. This economic integration has prompted a 'Europeanisation' of British politics which can be seen in the changed activities of central government, local authorities, political parties and pressure groups. Support for the European Community is growing in Britain, but lags behind that in most other member states.

Yet Britain remains a reluctant European. There are many reasons for this. Although trade links with the Commonwealth are no longer strong there are still social, cultural and sporting bonds. The fact that the Australians feel obliged to thrash the English at cricket every few years is one of the more unfortunate manifestations of old associations. Britain also maintains more sizeable trading and cultural links with America and Japan than with any one Community member. The legacies of superpower status and of a global, rather than regional, role can also be seen in Britain's continued possession of nuclear weapons and retention of a permanent seat – and veto – on the UN Security Council.

Britain's tradition comprises an 'expansive' rather than a 'pooled' sovereignty. The British have found it particularly hard to come to terms with their changed status in the world. Many argue that Britain's greatness is in the past, and that the challenge of the modern era is to respond to patterns of interdependence that increasingly link Britain to the Community. However, historical and political analysis cannot be reduced to a series of trade (or other) statistics. A range of factors tempers British enthusiasm for European integration and generates British reluctance.

NOTES

1 M Thatcher, *Britain and Europe: Text of the Prime Minister's Speech at Bruges on 20 September 1988* (Conservative Political Centre, London, 1988).
2 J Pinder, 'Positive Integration and Negative Integration: Some Problems of Economic Union in the EC', in M Hodges (ed), *European Integration* (Penguin, Harmondsworth, 1970), 124-50.
3 N Ridley, *My Style of Government* (Harper Collins, London, 1992), p.136.
4 S Mazey and J Richardson, *Lobbying in the European Community* (Oxford University Press, Oxford, 1993).
5 Trades Union Congress, *Europe 1992: Maximising the Benefits, Minimising the Costs* (TUC, London, 1988).
6 M Hewstone, *Understanding Attitudes to the European Community: A Socio-Psychological Study in Four Member States* (Cambridge University Press, Cambridge, 1986).

CONCLUSION

Britain's reluctance to 'integrate' and join a supranational order has underpinned its relationship with the Community both prior to and since accession. Despite this, Britain is manifestly becoming increasingly European. Consequently, the direction taken by the Community in the 1990s is of great importance to British people. Indeed, opponents of European integration find it hard to outline a credible alternative role for Britain outside the Community. If the debate about membership really is resolved – and it seems reasonable to assume that it is – two key questions arise. How influential can Britain be in shaping the European Community in the 1990s? And can Britain, as John Major hopes, move to the heart of Europe?

'OLD' AND 'NEW' EUROPE

In the mid 1990s the EC faces a similar dilemma to that which it faced at its inception in the early 1950s: what to do about Germany. The clear Cold War divide between West and East Germany symbolised the ideological fault-line that shaped 'old' Europe. Franco-German rapprochement was central to the process of supranational integration that 'pooled' sovereignty within the EC in a bid to cast aside nationalistic enmities and move towards a politically and economically integrated Europe.

Following the collapse of the Soviet bloc the EC must respond to the challenges of the 'new' Europe which has a reunified Germany at the core of a much changed European state system. Other factors that will shape the 'new' Europe are the Maastricht Treaty, its plan for European union, and political responses to the turmoil created by the ERM crisis of July to August 1993.

BRITAIN AT THE HEART OF EUROPE?

Two alternative scenarios for the Community in the 1990s can be envisaged. One, a looser, more intergovernmental Community accords with Britain's long-standing preferences. The other, a continuation along the integrative path outlined in the Maastricht Treaty, does not. Under each scenario, John Major's attempt to locate Britain at the heart of Europe seems implausible.

The first scenario posits that post-Maastricht turmoil in Europe will fatally undermine federal aspirations and induce a centrifugalism which generates a wider, more intergovernmental Community centred around the single market. Employment of the principle of subsidiarity, as defined by the British, could also see the repatriation of powers from supranational to national level. Such a Community would accord with long-held British preferences. However, even within such an arrangement the Germans, the strongest power in Europe, would be the dominant force. Widening would in fact reinforce this dominance by drawing in Scandinavian, central and east European countries which are increasingly dependent on the German economy. It would also tilt the geographical axis of the Community eastwards, and take it yet further from Britain's sphere of real influence. The European power with greatest influence over the Community's destiny would be incorporated into only loose structures of collective management at supranational level.

The second scenario posits pursuit of the Maastricht path to European Union, though at a slower pace and perhaps with what has been termed 'variable geometry' (which means that some countries integrate more rapidly than others). This scenario takes into account the important political ambition that underpins the EC, and which has made it far more than just a free-trade arrangement. A core group of member states (Germany, France, Italy and the Benelux countries) has long held a commitment to European integration. The Franco-German partnership has been central to this process, and despite the severe difficulties it experienced during the ERM crisis can be expected to continue. French concern about a restoration of German power has not been eliminated by development of the 'new' Europe. If anything it has increased as a result of reunification.

A principal feature of this post-Maastricht scenario is emergence of a two-speed Europe with a core group of member states, led by Germany, pushing on to EMU. Britain would be unlikely to participate in such a venture. In addition, a wider Community, with the accession of the Norwegians, Finns, Austrians and Swedes, could generate pressure – as it did in the 1980s – for further deepening. Maastricht is to be reviewed in 1996 when Community institutions and policies will be considered. Steps may then be taken to cut the 'democratic deficit'. Possible changes are an increase in the power of supranational institutions such as the European Parliament, and extension of the range of issues covered by QMV. The intergovernmental CFSP and JHA 'pillars' of Maastricht could also be incorporated within the supranational Community method of decision-making. It is well-nigh impossible to imagine Britain at the heart of such a scenario, even if the Conservatives lose office.

This post-Maastricht scenario has at its core a centripetal integrative impetus which acknowledges the formidable 'logic' that underpins integration and is closely linked to the aspirations of core member states. It guarantees, of course, neither the success nor the desirability of the federal goal.

THE BRITISH DILEMMA

Of these two alternative scenarios only one is in accord with stated British preferences. However, the dilemma for the British government is that even its preferred scenario would be unlikely to place Britain at the heart of the Community. John Major's dream is apparently unattainable in any conceivable EC future.

Nevertheless, the scope and direction of European integration remains a matter of great concern to the British. To the dismay of those bored rigid by Maastricht, debates about Europe will not go away in the 1990s. Yet it seems unlikely that Britain will ever be central to the process of European integration.

For a variety of reasons reviewed in Chapters 3 and 7, Britain's reputation as a reluctant European is justified. It is often by choice that Britain has been peripheral to European integration. A wider Community in the 1990s would accord with British preferences but is likely to consolidate German pre-eminence. It will not move Britain to the heart of the Community. A deeper EC which sustains the political intent that has been central to European integration would not accord with British preferences. It too will leave Britain on the margins of the EC, and is likely to increase British reluctance.

APPENDIX

Appendix 1 Chronology of main events in EC development, 1948-93

1948

March   Brussels Treaty establishes a collective defence organisation comprising France, Britain and the Benelux countries.

April   Organisation for European Economic Cooperation (OEEC) established with 16 member states.

May   Congress of Europe meets in The Hague.

1949

April   Treaty of Washington signed by 12 member states establishes NATO.

May   Council of Europe established.

1950

May   French foreign minister Robert Schuman puts forward plan for a coal and steel community.

1951

April   Treaty of Paris establishes the European Coal and Steel Community (ECSC) with six members (France, West Germany, Italy and the Benelux countries).

1954

August   French National Assembly rejects plans for a European Defence Community (EDC). West European Union (WEU) established as an intergovernmental collective defence organisation.

1955

June   Messina conference of ECSC foreign ministers discusses further integration.

1957

March   Treaties of Rome establish the European Economic Community (EEC) and Euratom with six founder members (France, West Germany, Italy and the Benelux countries).

1959

July   Stockholm Convention establishes the European Free Trade Area (EFTA) with seven members (Austria, Britain, Denmark, Norway, Portugal, Sweden and Switzerland).

1963

January   General de Gaulle vetoes Britain's first application for EC membership.

1965

July   France begins a boycott of Community institutions in protest at supranational developments.

1966

January   Luxembourg Accord agrees use of national vetoes and allows normal Community decision-making procedures to resume.

1968

July   EEC Customs Union established, with the result that all internal duties and quotas are removed and the Common External Tariff is put in place for goods from outside the Community.

1969

July   Pompidou announces that he does not oppose British membership.

1970

April   Community budgetary process established.

1972

January   Britain, Denmark, Ireland and Norway sign Treaties of Accession to the EC.

September   Norwegian people vote 'No' to Community membership.

1973

January   Accession of Britain, Denmark and Ireland.

1975

June   Referendum on British membership of the Community produces a two to one vote in favour of continued participation.

1979

June   First direct elections to the European Parliament.

1981

January   Accession of Greece.

1984

June   Second set of direct elections to the European Parliament. Fontainebleau summit produces a budget rebate for Britain.

1985

June   Commission publishes its White Paper, *Completing the Internal Market*.

1986

January   Accession of Spain and Portugal.

June   Single European Act (SEA) establishes plan for completion of the single market by the end of 1992.

1988

February   Brussels European Council meeting agrees a five-year financial perspective for the Community which raises the budget from 1.14 per cent of member states' GNP to 1.20 per cent.

1989

April   Delors Report presents a three-stage plan for EMU.

June   Third set of direct elections to the European Parliament.

September- Soviet bloc crumbles, beginning with the appointment of a

December   non-Communist Prime Minister in Poland and ending with the overthrow of Ceaucescu in Romania.

December   Strasbourg European Council meeting adopts the Social Charter and agrees to convene an intergovernmental conference on economic and monetary union (EMU). Both decisions are taken by eleven votes to one, with Britain the dissenter.

1990

October   Reunification of Germany leads to incorporation of the former GDR in the Community.

December   Intergovernmental conferences on economic and political union opened at the Rome European Council.

1991

December   Maastricht Summit agrees the Treaty on European Union which, amongst other things, gives the three-stage plan for EMU legal effect.

1992

June   The Danes vote 'No' to Maastricht by 51 per cent to 49 per cent.

September Sterling forced out of the ERM.
           The French referendum returns a petit oui to Maastricht by 51 per cent to 49 per cent.

December   Edinburgh European Council meeting agrees a financial perspective to take the Community through to the end of the century, by which time the Community budget will amount to 1.27 per cent of member states' GNP.

1993

August   Heavy speculative pressure on the ERM leads to a widening of its bands to 15 per cent.
           Britain ratifies the Maastricht Treaty.

A BRIEF GUIDE TO FURTHER READING

There are many good books on the historical development of the Community. D Urwin, *The Community of Europe* (Longman, London, 1991) provides an excellent introduction. For detailed analysis of specific events in Community history, see R Pryce (ed) *The Dynamics of European Union* (Croom Helm, London, 1987). J Story (ed) *The New Europe* (Blackwell, Oxford, 1992) assesses the impact on the Community of major events in the 1980s and early 1990s (such as the end of the Cold War and plans for EMU).

For a good account of the various European organisations that have emerged in the post-war era see C Archer, *Organizing Western Europe* (Edward Arnold, London, 1990). Also see J Lodge, *Integration and Cooperation in Europe* (Routledge, London, 1992).

The best book on the institutional structure of the EC is N Nugent, *The Government and Politics of the European Community*, second edition (Macmillan, London, 1991). On Community policies see D Swann, *The Economics of the Common Market*, seventh edition (Penguin, Harmondsworth, 1992) and L Tsoukalis, *The New European Economy* (Oxford University Press, Oxford, 1991).

On Britain and the EC, S George, *An Awkward Partner: Britain in the European Community* (Oxford University Press, Oxford, 1991) gives a good overview of British government policies. S Greenwood, *Britain and European Cooperation since 1945* (Blackwell, Oxford, 1992) looks more closely at events prior to accession.

Academic journals are good sources of up-to-date information on developments in the EC. Many journals contain articles relating to the EC, though two are particularly valuable. The *Journal of Common Market Studies* focuses exclusively on the Community and carries an annual review of EC activities. *International Affairs* also has a strong focus on events in Europe.

For those seeking more detailed information a number of academic libraries contain European Documentation Centres within which a large amount of material on Community activities can be found.

INDEX

Acheson, Dean 26
Amalgamated Union of Engineering
  Workers (AUEW) 99
Association of South East Asian Nations
  (ASEAN) 1
Austria
  EFTA membership 8, 25
  prospects for EC membership 84, 104

Bangemann, Martin 43
Barber case 80
Belgium
  EC membership 2
  subsidiarity 14
Benelux Customs Union (1948) 21
Benn, Tony 31, 96
Brandt, Willy 29, 62
Britain
  attitude to social policy 62-6
  attitude to subsidiarity 39
  budget rebate 17, 29-30
  Commonwealth ties 28-9
  constitutional implications of
    EC membership 92-4
  distrust of supranationalism 1, 19,27-8
  ERM membership 60-1
  impact of EC environmental
    policy 81-2
  impact of EC on central
    government 93-4
  impact of EC on local
    government 94-5
  joins EC 2, 29-31
  joins EFTA 8, 25
  party attitudes 95-8
  Presidency of EC 47, 52-3
  pressure groups and the EC 98-9
  public opinion 99-100
  referendum on EC membership 31-2
  single market implementation 37
  social policy 62-6
  'special relationship' with USA 28
  subsidiarity 39
  trade patterns 91-2
  White Paper on EC membership 30, 92
Brittan, Sir Leon 42-3
Broek, Hans van den 43
Brussels Treaty (1948) 20
Budgen, Nicholas 95

Bulgaria 86
Bundesbank 60-2

Callaghan, James
  as Foreign Secretary 31
  as Prime Minister 32-3
Cassis de Dijon 37
Christopherson, Henning 43
Churchill, Winston 23, 28
Cockfield, Lord 35-6, 43
Cold War 7
Committee for the Study of
  Economic and Monetary Union 59-60
Committee of Permanent
  Representatives (COREPER) 47-8, 94
Committee of Professional Agricultural
  Associations (COPA) 54, 74
Committee of the Regions 94
Common Agricultural Policy (CAP)
  founding principles 24-5
  operation and reform 73-7
Common External Tariff 25
Commonwealth 28-9
Confederation of British Industry (CBI) 98
Congress of Europe 21
Conservative party
  attitudes to EC membership
    30, 39-40, 95-6
  attitudes to EC social policy 63-4
  in European Parliament 50-1
Council of Europe 21
Council of Ministers
  British Presidency 47-8, 52-3
  responsibilities 24, 41, 46-8
  voting procedures 35
Cyprus 87-8
Czechoslovakia 20, 86

de Gaulle, Charles
  attitude to British membership of EC
    25, 27-9
  suspicion of supranationalism
    15-6, 46, 95
Delors, Jacques
  Commission President 42-3
  EC integration 17
  single market 35
  social policy 62-3
  subsidiarity 13
  trade unions 99
Democratic Unionist Party (DUP) 98
Denmark
  joins EC 2, 30
  joins EFTA 8, 25
  Maastricht referenda 9, 55
  single market implementation 37